FACTS AT YOUR
FINGERTIPS

# ENDANGERED ANIMALS
# BIRDS

BROWN
BEAR
BOOKS

## Published by Brown Bear Books Limited

4877 N. Circulo Bujia
Tucson, AZ 85718
USA

and

First Floor
9-17 St. Albans Place
London N1 ONX
UK

© 2011 Brown Bear Books Ltd

### Library of Congress Cataloging-in-Publication Data

Birds / edited by Tim Harris.
   p. cm. – (Facts at your fingertips. Endangered animals)
Includes bibliographical references and index.
 Summary: "Describes various birds that are endangered and at risk of becoming extinct. Data Sheet sidebars and maps accompany the text"–Provided by publisher.
 ISBN 978-1-936333-31-8 (library binding)
1. Rare birds–Juvenile literature. 2. Endangered species–Juvenile literature. I. Harris, Tim. II. Title. III. Series.

QL676.7.B35 2012
598.168–dc22

2010053975

ISBN-13 978-1-936333-31-8

**Editorial Director:** Lindsey Lowe
**Editor:** Tim Harris
**Creative Director:** Jeni Child
**Designer:** Lynne Lennon
**Children's Publisher:** Anne O'Daly
**Production Director:** Alastair Gourlay

Printed in the United States of America

In this book you will see the following key at top left of each entry. The key shows the level of threat faced by each animal, as judged by the International Union for the Conservation of Nature (IUCN).

| | |
|---|---|
| **EX** | Extinct |
| **EW** | Extinct in the Wild |
| **CR** | Critically Endangered |
| **EN** | Endangered |
| **VU** | Vulnerable |
| **NT** | Near Threatened |
| **LC** | Least Concern |
| **O** | Other (this includes Data Deficient and Not Evaluated) |

For a few animals that have not been evaluated since 2001, the old status of Lower Risk still applies and this is shown by the letters **LR** on the key.

For more information on Categories of Threat, see pp. 54–57.

## Picture Credits

**Abbreviations:** c=center; t=top; l=left; r=right.

**Cover Images**
Front: *Flamingo,* Thinkstock/istockphoto
Back: *Red kite,* Public Domain/Thomas Kraft

AL: Dm Oarer & E Parer-Cook; 10; **BCC:** John Cancalosi 34–35, 43. J. Grande 25, Phil Savoie 17; **FLPA:** Tui De Roy 57; **Photolibrary Group:** Animals Animals 29, Robin Bush 6t, 37, Mark Jones 8, Steve Littlewood 14–15, Stephen Mills 21, Stan Osolinski 11 inset, 39, Norbert Rosing 59–59; Jorge Sierra 26–27, Tony Tilford 53, Robert Tyrrell 45; **Photoshot:** Laurie Campbell/NHPA 4, Martin Harvey/NHPA 6b, Daniel Heuclin/NHPA 23; **PEP:** John Bracegirdle 19, Ken Lucas 33; **Public Domain:** Thomas Kraft 1; **Windrush Photos:** Rene Pop 50–51

Artwork © Brown Bear Books Ltd

*Brown Bear Books has made every attempt to contact the copyright holder. If you have any information please email smortimer@brownbearbooks.co.uk*

# CONTENTS

| | |
|---|---|
| What is a Bird? | **4** |
| Northern Brown Kiwi | **8** |
| Galápagos Penguin | **10** |
| Bermuda Petrel | **12** |
| Andean Flamingo | **14** |
| Northern Bald Ibis | **16** |
| White-headed Duck | **18** |
| Nene | **20** |
| Philippine Eagle | **22** |
| Spanish Imperial Eagle | **24** |
| Red Kite | **26** |
| California Condor | **28** |
| Mauritius Kestrel | **30** |
| Whooping Crane | **32** |
| Takahe | **34** |
| Kakapo | **36** |
| Hyacinth Macaw | **38** |
| Pink Pigeon | **40** |
| Spotted Owl | **42** |
| Bee Hummingbird | **44** |
| Regent Honeyeater | **46** |
| Blue Bird of Paradise | **48** |
| Raso Lark | **50** |
| Gouldian Finch | **52** |
| *Categories of Threat* | **54** |
| *Organizations* | **58** |
| *Glossary/Further Research* | **62** |
| *Index* | **64** |

# What is a Bird?

**The house sparrow** *is one of the world's most successful birds, yet even this adaptable species has declined in places.*

**B**irds are among the most successful of all groups of animals, found everywhere from the bleak icy wastes of the Arctic and Antarctic and the tops of the highest mountains to baking-hot deserts, and from the most remote oceanic islands and the interior of vast jungles to farmland and city streets.

Crucial to this success has been their mastery of flight. The whole body of a bird is adapted to this end. Its forearms have become modified to form wings, the bony tail has been replaced by a fan of feathers, many of the bones are hollow and light in weight, the jaws are modified into a lightweight horny beak instead of heavy, tooth-filled jaws, and there is a system of air-filled sacs within much of the body. Laying large, yolk-rich eggs enables birds to avoid carrying around a heavy embryo within the body, and they have well developed brains and acute senses.

Birds also have superbly efficient blood-circulatory and respiratory systems, enabling many species to fly far, fast, or high, as their needs dictate. It is birds that hold the record for long-distance migration; many Arctic terns regularly make a round trip of 25,000 miles (40,200 km) between the Arctic and the Antarctic each year. They also hold records for flight speed—the peregrine falcon is the fastest-moving living thing under its own power, reaching speeds of 117 miles per hour (188 km/h). And birds can fly at considerable altitudes—a Rüppell's griffon vulture collided with an aircraft at 37,000 feet (11,300 m).

The key to their superb powers of flight is the evolution of feathers, which distinguish birds from all other animals. These structures, made of keratin—a material similar to that found in your hair and nails—form the plumage of the bird, which helps it fly and provides insulation, colors for camouflage or communication, waterproofing, and other uses.

Considering the limitations imposed on them by acquiring the power of flight, birds are remarkably varied in appearance and lifestyle. They have a much greater species diversity than other groups of vertebrates apart from fish, with almost 9,800 species—over twice as many species as mammals.

## Flightlessness

Although the great majority of birds can fly, certain groups or individual species have abandoned flight during their evolutionary history. Examples include the ratites (flightless running birds, whose living representatives include the ostrich and kiwis), the penguins, the kakapo (pp. 36–37), and extinct birds such as the great auk and dodo.

Originally this strategy was a neat way of saving energy for birds that lived on islands or other places where there were no land predators and so no need to fly to escape them. But flightlessness also meant that many species succumbed to predators such as cats and rats introduced by settlers.

## The History of Birds

Birds evolved from reptiles over 160 million years ago. These two great groups, or classes, of animals share many characteristics, including details of their skulls, ear bones, and lower jaws, and similarities between their eggs.

Although there has been disagreement about which group of reptiles gave rise to birds, most researchers think that they evolved directly from small, agile, lightweight theropod dinosaurs called coelurosaurs that ran on their hind legs.

## Adaptive Radiation

The rapid evolution of flowering plants and the insects that depended on them paved the way for an explosion of opportunities for fruit-eating, nectar-feeding, and insect-eating birds, especially of the great group known as the passerines (perching birds, including songbirds). Today passerines make up over half of all bird species in the world.

By 5 to 10 million years ago birds had diversified into a great range of different genera, including many that still have representatives today. Living birds range in size from the tiny bee hummingbird (pp. 44–45), smaller than some insects, to the mighty ostrich, males of which can be 9 feet (3 m) tall. This impressive natural diversity is being diminished as humans affect the survival of bird species.

## Why Are Birds at Risk?

Birds are threatened today by a variety of factors, over 99 percent of them the result of human activities. The effects of habitat destruction and degradation are the major threat to 85 percent of all threatened species. The next most important threat comes from direct exploitation, affecting 31 percent of the total. It is mainly due to hunting for food, as with the Baikal teal, and the trapping of many millions of birds each year for the cage-bird trade, both local and international. The latter threat affects some groups of birds particularly seriously, notably the parrots, such as the salmon-crested cockatoo.

The third most serious threat is from the introduction by humans of animals, especially to islands. Almost all extinctions of bird species since 1800 have been of island birds whose lack of natural defenses made them easy targets for introduced predators. Today a quarter of all threatened species face this threat; the Guam rail became extinct in the wild because of predation by introduced snakes. Other species are affected by habitat degradation caused by goats and other grazing animals as well as by alien plants that crowd out the natural vegetation.

Diseases can have devastating effects on birds. Avian malaria, spread by introduced mosquitoes, was at least partly responsible for the extinction of many species of endemic Hawaiian birds.

Other threats include pollution, acid rain, and oil spills. In the longer term the impact of climate change, due mainly to human-induced global warming, will pose an increasing threat to many birds; changes in ocean currents are already having a profound effect on some seabirds, such as

**Prehistoric birds** (numbered in order of age) include toothed diving seabirds (1, 2), giant flightless predators (3, 5), ancestors of vultures (4) and flamingos (6), and the largest known flying birds (7).

the Galápagos penguin (pp. 10–11). Seabirds are also threatened by overfishing, and huge numbers are killed when they are accidentally caught on the hooks of longlines, as with the wandering albatross. Poisoning—both deliberate and accidental—also affects threatened birds such as the Cape griffon vulture, as do wars and the disturbance of wary birds—especially at their breeding colonies—by tourists, ramblers, climbers, watersports enthusiasts, and even conservationists.

## The Present Situation

Of the 10,027 or so species of birds in the world today, 1,240 species—almost one in eight—are threatened with global extinction unless something is done to save them. Of them 190 are Critically Endangered. A further 372 species are Endangered, another 678 species are Vulnerable, and 838 species are Lower Risk, near threatened. Many subspecies are also in danger. The Cape Verde race of red kite (p. 26), for example, is now extinct.

Already over 120 other species of birds are known to have become extinct since the last dodo died in the 1660s—almost all of them as a result of human impact. Given the natural rate of evolution, we would expect one bird species to go extinct every 100 years, so 103 in the last 200 years is 50 times the expected rate.

Each year one or two new bird species are discovered by

**Birds face many threats,** *including introduced predators, as with this brown kiwi (above), and pollution. This jackass penguin (left) is covered in oil from a sunken cargo boat.*

biologists, mainly in the tropics. Many are rare, with tiny ranges and in threatened habitats, and so were in peril even before they were known to science.

Few birds are found over all or most of the world; the barn owl and cattle egret are the only species to have been recorded on every continent. Worst off are the parrots, with more species globally threatened than any other family. Trapping for the cage-bird trade is a major threat at both local and worldwide levels, made even more serious by habitat loss.

## Where the Dangers Lie

Of the 12 countries that contain the greatest concentrations of threatened bird species, seven are in the Americas. The highest densities of threatened birds occur in the Atlantic forests of Brazil and the northern Andes of Colombia and Ecuador.

Almost half of all the extinctions of birds recorded since 1650 have been from species living in Oceania— the islands of the central and south Pacific Ocean and adjacent seas, including Australia, New Zealand, New Guinea, New Caledonia, the Solomons, Fiji, and the rest of Melanesia, Micronesia, and Polynesia.

Although there are relatively few threatened birds exclusively found in Europe and the Middle East, most of the species at risk in these regions make yearly migrations between summer breeding grounds and wintering areas. In many cases that pattern of behavior exposes them to a wide range of threats.

## Most-Threatened Habitats

Threatened birds are mainly restricted to specific habitats: 74 percent depend almost completely on a single type of habitat. Of them forest birds form 75 percent, of which 93 percent are found only in the tropics, and 82 percent are restricted to moist forests.

**Percentage of birds threatened**
- 0–2
- 2–3
- 3–7
- 7–42
- no data

The next most important habitats are grasslands, scrublands, and savannas, with 32 percent of all the world's threatened species. Wetlands too, especially freshwater ones, are also of great significance, holding 12 percent of all threatened birds.

## Conservation

There are many reasons for conserving birds. They are fascinating creatures that have inspired people over the centuries, and people care about them. Most importantly, birds are good indicators of the state of our environment; places that are rich in bird species are also rich in the biodiversity of other classes of animals. So where birds are threatened with extinction is often a good indication of general biodiversity loss and damage to ecosystems.

The task of saving species such as the spoon-billed sandpiper whose journeys take them across the globe, recognizing no international boundaries, requires careful coordination of efforts among nations. BirdLife International—a global partnership of conservation organizations in over 100 countries—is one organization that is dedicated to saving birds and their habitats.

**Threatened birds worldwide.** *Less than 5 percent of the earth's land surface contains almost 75 percent of threatened bird species.*

Since the greatest threat is habitat destruction and degradation, BirdLife International has created a program that will identify about 20,000 Important Bird Areas (IBAs) throughout the world. The most effective way of saving threatened birds is to protect such sites before they suffer threats; but sometimes—as in Madagascar, Hawaii, or New Zealand—the problems caused by habitat loss, introduced animals, and other factors mean that the affected species require intensive and costly conservation programs.

Another problem facing conservationists is that they simply do not have enough information about the range, numbers, or ecology of many threatened bird species. Gaining such knowledge is an important part of their work. Knowledge about threatened birds and their habitats is also vital for persuading governments, business interests, and other decision-makers to act in ways that will benefit the birds and for the drawing up and enforcement of agreements at local, national, or international levels.

# Northern Brown Kiwi

### *Apteryx mantelli*

*The mainland populations of the unique northern brown kiwi—found only in New Zealand—have suffered huge declines in the 20th century, mainly due to plundering by introduced predators.*

**The female northern brown kiwi** *lays large eggs: Each egg weighs as much as 20 percent of her body weight.*

With its shaggy, hairlike plumage, a plump, round body, a lack of visible tail or wings, and an ability to track down food in the dead of night, kiwis resemble nocturnal mammals rather than typical birds. Like many mammals, they also rest and shelter their young in burrows and mark their boundaries with strong-smelling droppings; the bristly modified feathers at the base of the bill serve as whiskers for feeling in the dark. Isolated for millions of years on New Zealand—where there are no native mammals except bats—the brown kiwi has occupied a niche that elsewhere would be filled by a mammal.

Kiwis are the smallest living ratites—a group of flightless birds that includes the ostrich, rheas, cassowaries, and the emu, none of which are nocturnal. Until recently ornithologists recognized three species of kiwi: the little spotted kiwi, the brown kiwi, and the great spotted kiwi. Genetic research has led to the brown kiwi being split into two distinct species, the northern brown kiwi and the tokoeka of a few areas in South Island. The Maori name *kiwi* comes from the shrill call of males, which punctuates the night, especially during the breeding season.

## Long-Term Decline

Northern brown kiwis were once widespread throughout North Island. Although they were hunted by the Maori—who had colonized New Zealand from the Pacific by the 12th century—this probably had little effect on overall numbers. It was not until the European settlers arrived in the mid-19th century that persecution of the birds began in earnest, as hunters

tried to satisfy the demand for kiwi plumage by the clothing trade. A law banning the hunting, capture, or killing of kiwis was passed in 1908, but the pace of land clearance for agriculture and settlements destroyed much of the kiwi's forest habitat. The birds' fate was further sealed by the introduction of predatory mammals such as cats, dogs, and stoats. As a result of the combined threats, large-scale losses of brown kiwis occurred.

Researchers think that numbers of brown kiwis have fallen by at least 90 percent over the last 100 years and continue to decline at about 6 percent every year (in studied sites). This represents the halving of the population each decade. However, the species' overall decline is probably below 80 percent, thanks to the stability of the populations introduced to islands where predators are removed—and also to effective predator control in mainland sites.

The main threat facing the northern brown kiwi is still introduced predators, especially since it evolved with no native predators. At least 94 percent of kiwi chicks die before they reach breeding age (about 14 months for males and two years for females). Half of this mortality is due to predation. The other main cause of decline is the clearance of native forest, which threatens small, isolated populations. Many

**The northern brown kiwi** *is nocturnal and has tiny, poorly developed eyes that enable it to see only a few yards ahead. Unusually for a bird, it detects its prey by smell.*

kiwis also used to die in traps set to catch predators or possums; animals reached plague proportions in some areas. Today this is avoided by raising traps above the ground so that the kiwis do not stumble upon them.

## Conservation

Conservationists have an accurate picture of kiwi populations thanks to an intensive, nationally coordinated program of monitoring. By culling introduced predators and by removing eggs and hand-rearing the young to an age when they can fend off attacks, key populations have been helped. Continued protection is needed to save the northern brown kiwi.

## DATA PANEL

**Northern brown kiwi**

*Apteryx mantelli*

**Family:** Apterygidae

**World population:** About 35,000 birds

**Distribution:** North Island in Northland; Coromandel Peninsula from Gisborne to northern Ruahine Range, and Tongariro to Taranaki. Introduced to Little Barrier, Kawau, and Pounui Islands.

**Habitat:** Subtropical and temperate forests; regenerating forest, shrubland, pine plantations, and pastureland

**Size:** Length: 16 in (40 cm). Weight: male 3–6.5 lb (1.4–3 kg); female 4.5–8 lb (2–3.8 kg)

**Form:** Bird the size of a small dog; small head; long, slightly downcurved bill with bristles at base; long neck (usually drawn in); rotund body covered with coarse, hairlike plumage that is dark gray-brown with red-brown streaks; rudimentary wing stubs in plumage; strong legs; 4 toes on each foot

**Diet:** Invertebrates in soil and leaf litter, especially earthworms, spiders, and insects; also fruit, seeds, and leaves

**Breeding:** Female lays 1 or 2 very large eggs in August–September in burrow or natural cavity; egg(s) incubated by male for 11–12 weeks; chick(s) independent at 14–20 days; fully grown by 20 months

**Related endangered species:** Great spotted kiwi (*Apteryx haastii*) VU; little spotted kiwi (*A. owenii*) NT; tokoeka (*A. australis*) VU

**Status:** IUCN EN

North Island

NEW ZEALAND

South Island

# Galápagos Penguin

## *Spheniscus mendiculus*

*The only species of penguin to live on the Equator, the portly Galápagos penguin breeds on at least five of the Galápagos Islands. Because of its restricted range and very small population, a sharp decline in numbers is particularly disturbing.*

Penguins are normally associated with cold habitats in and around Antarctica, although several species have ranges that include warmer climates. The Humboldt penguin, for instance, breeds in coastal Chile and Peru. However, the Galápagos penguin—a close relative of the Humboldt—is the only species that lives entirely within the tropics, on at least five islands of the Galápagos group. Life at such latitudes is challenging for the birds, since their insulating plumage, underlying fat, and specialized blood heat exchange—all adaptations for surviving in very cold water—make it difficult for them to cope with the tropical heat when on land. Temperatures in the Galápagos Islands can rise to more than 104°F (40°C).

## Adaptations to Heat

In order to survive the heat, the Galápagos penguin has various anatomical and behavioral adaptations. It is one of the smallest penguin species, and the smaller an animal, the greater its surface area relative to its total size. Consequently, the Galápagos penguin has a large surface area from which to dissipate (lose) heat when on land. Heat loss is made easier by its having shorter feathers than any other species of penguin.

When ashore, the adults seek shade. They lose more heat by increasing the blood flow to their flippers, feet, and bare facial patches. The flippers are proportionately larger than those of cold-climate penguins, increasing the area where heat exchange can take place. The animals' blood supply can also bypass the heat-transfer system that helps maintain their body temperature in cold water. Galápagos penguins often breed in rock crevices and caves, such as lava tubes (natural tunnels in lava flows) that shade the birds and their chicks from the sun.

## Major Threats

The Galápagos penguin depends directly on the surrounding ocean for its survival.

---

## DATA PANEL

**Galápagos penguin**

*Spheniscus mendiculus*

**Family:** Spheniscidae

**World population:** Fluctuates greatly; currently estimated at 1,500 individuals

**Distribution:** Galápagos Islands, Ecuador

**Habitat:** Breeds on low-lying areas of coastal, volcanic desert, rarely more than 55 yards (50 m) inland; feeds around upwellings of cool, nutrient-rich inshore waters

**Size:** Length: 19–21 in (48–53 cm); height: 14 in (35 cm). Weight: average 3.8–5.7 lb (1.7–2.6 kg)

**Form:** Small with black head; white stripes on face; black to brownish back and tail; chin and underparts white; variable pattern of black spots and irregular black bands on breast; flippers brown-black above, white below; male more boldly marked. Juveniles have grayish upperparts and lack distinctive face pattern

**Diet:** Schools of ocean fish, including sardines and mullet. Possibly crustaceans

**Breeding:** Breeds at any time, in small colonies or singly, when food supply is adequate; nests in lava tubes, rock crevices, or caves, at least partly shaded from the sun; 2 white eggs laid per breeding attempt; pair shares incubation that lasts 5–6 weeks; young leave nest at 8.5–9 weeks

**Related endangered species**: Nine other penguin species are threatened, including African penguin (*Spheniscus demersus*) EN; Humboldt penguin (*S. humboldti*) VU; erect-crested penguin (*Eudyptes sclateri*) EN; Snares penguin (*E. robustus*) VU

**Status:** IUCN EN

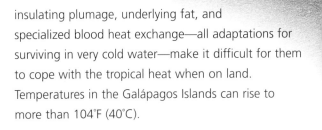

COSTA RICA
PANAMA
COLOMBIA
Galápagos Islands (Ecuador)
ECUADOR
PERU

The Cromwell Current, an upwelling of cool, nutrient-rich water, maintains the fish stocks that the penguins rely on for food. The current is susceptible to a periodic climatic event called the El Niño Southern Oscillation (ENSO). Records show that a population of 3,400 penguins declined by 77 percent between 1982 and 1983—an ENSO year that adversely affected the Cromwell Current, reducing fish stocks and causing thousands of birds to starve. It is likely that more females than males died, which would have slowed the recovery of the population. Another ENSO event in 1997 caused a further decline of 66 percent.

Galápagos penguins are known to be slow breeders, the birth rate averaging out at only 1.3 chicks per year. In ENSO years the entire population can fail to breed at all. The animals also have a restricted breeding range, with about 95 percent nesting on just two islands. Chicks and eggs are vulnerable to natural predators such as rice rats, snakes, and crabs. More serious threats are posed by introduced predators, including feral dogs, cats, and brown and black rats, which kill adults and chicks.

**Galápagos penguins** *feed on the rich fish stocks around the Galápagos Islands. The small, dapper bird has large flippers and feet that help it dissipate body heat.*

A tenfold increase in the permanent human population of the Galápagos in the last 40 years has led to disturbance of breeding sites and an expansion of coastal fisheries. Penguins are caught in nets and suffer from competition for fish stocks. Tourism adds to disruption; visitors come to look at the birds.

To ensure the continued survival of the Galápagos penguin, controls on fisheries, oil spills, human disturbance, and the introduction of mammalian predators are urgently required, as are scientific studies of the penguins to help increase their breeding success rate. Most importantly, we need to cut fossil fuel emissions to reduce global warming, which is likely to increase ENSO events.

# Bermuda Petrel

### *Pterodroma cahow*

*The story of this graceful seabird is an extraordinary saga of rediscovery after hundreds of years of presumed extinction, followed by a steady increase in numbers due to the efforts of conservationists. The population is still dangerously small, however, and the bird continues to face several threats.*

Bermuda is made up of about 150 small islands in the northwestern Atlantic Ocean, 750 miles (1,200 km) off the east coast of the United States. As well as serving as a useful stopover site in spring and fall for windblown migrants, it is home to one of the world's rarest seabirds, the Bermuda petrel.

Also known as the cahow in imitation of its eerie mating calls, the bird is one of the so-called gadfly petrels of the *Pterodroma* genus. They are graceful, long-winged birds, fast in flight, alternating bursts of rapid wingbeats with long glides. They rarely alight on the water, feeding on the wing by seizing small sea creatures such as squid from just below the water's surface with their sharp, hooked bills. In contrast, they are awkward on land, managing only a shuffling walk due to the position of their feet at the back of their bodies. To avoid the attentions of predators, the birds visit their colonies only under cover of darkness.

## Lost and Found

Bermuda remained uninhabited until 1609, when an English expedition was shipwrecked there. At the time the islands teemed with seabirds, including vast numbers of Bermuda petrels. Soon, however, settlers arrived in force, bringing with them pigs, rats, and other animals that raided the petrels' nesting burrows. To make matters worse, the settlers themselves also caught and ate huge numbers of the birds, until by 1621 the species was thought to be extinct.

No specimens were recorded for more than 300 years, but then, miraculously, the bird turned up again. The first clue that it still existed came in 1906, when a dead petrel was found on Castle Island, one of the smallest in Bermuda. At first it was taken to be a previously unknown capped petrel from the

---

## DATA PANEL

### Bermuda petrel (cahow)

*Pterodroma cahow*

**Family:** Procellariidae

**World population:** About 250 birds

**Distribution:** Breeds on a few islets in Castle Harbor, Bermuda; outside the breeding season (mid-June–October) the birds live at sea, probably wandering across the Atlantic Ocean; has been recorded off North Carolina

**Habitat:** Breeds on rocky islets; spends nonbreeding season flying over open ocean

**Size:** Length: 15 in (38 cm); wingspan: 35 in (89 cm)

**Form:** Medium-sized, long-winged, short-tailed seabird with hooked black bill bearing nostrils in tubes on top; webbed feet set at hind end of body

**Diet:** Little known; probably mainly squid and crustaceans, plus some fish

**Breeding:** January to mid-June; colonies once nested in burrows in soil, but now use natural crevices in soft limestone and artificial burrows; single, large white egg is incubated for 7–8 weeks; young fledge in 13–14 weeks

**Related endangered species:** Thirty-five other petrel and shearwater species are threatened, and a further 2 are extinct. In the *Pterodroma* genus to which the Bermuda petrel belongs they include: Chatham Islands petrel (*Pterodroma axillaris*) EN; Galápagos petrel (*P. phaeopygia*) CR; Jamaica petrel (*P. caribbaea*) CR; black-capped petrel (*P. hasitata*) EN; Barau's petrel (*P. baraui*) EN; Trindade petrel (*P. arminjoniana*) VU; Atlantic petrel (*P. incerta*) EN; Murphy's petrel (*P. ultima*) NT

**Status:** IUCN EN

Caribbean region, but then in 1916 another individual turned up—and it seemed to fit 17th-century descriptions of the missing species. The clinching record came in 1931, when a bird that hit St. David's lighthouse was retrieved and identified as a Bermuda petrel. Another definite record was of an individual that struck a telephone pole in St. George, at the northeastern end of the main island.

The puzzle of where these birds came from remained, since none could be found nesting on any of the inhabited islands. In 1951 a search turned up 18 pairs of the petrels nesting on rocky islets in Castle Harbor, near St. George. The total area of these islets was only 2.4 acres (1 ha). Instead of nesting in burrows as they had done in the 17th century, the petrels were now using natural crevices created by water erosion of the soft limestone rock, since there was little soil on the islets.

*The Bermuda petrel was considered extinct for more than 300 years and was only rediscovered in the early years of the 20th century.*

## Building Up the Numbers

After its rediscovery the tiny breeding population was carefully observed. Worryingly, numbers increased only slightly in the early years; by 1961 there were still only 20 pairs. Like all other members of the tubenose order, which includes albatrosses and shearwaters as well as petrels, Bermuda petrels are slow breeders: Roosting birds lay a single egg, and the young take five or more years to become sexually mature.

Subsequently, research into the reasons for the petrels' poor productivity revealed that one problem facing the birds came in the shape of another seabird, the white-tailed tropicbird, which competed for the rock crevices where the petrels bred, killing the young in the nest after they hatched. Conservationists built artificial burrows for the petrels, but these too were attacked. Eventually, researchers solved the problem by fitting stone or wooden baffles over the burrow entrances that allowed the petrels to pass in but kept the bulkier tropicbirds out. This has had some success: The population is increasing, and breeding success is up to 25 percent from 5 percent in the 1950s.

Breeding numbers increased from their 1951 low to 71 pairs in 2005. However, a lingering threat comes from DDT and other pollutants, which become concentrated in the petrels' bodies and may be responsible for eggs that fail to hatch. The bright lights of a nearby airport and NASA tracking station also cause problems by disrupting the petrels' nighttime aerial courtship rituals. More worrying still is the risk of rising sea levels as a result of global warming—petrel burrows could flood as they did in the 1990s. Conservationists have replanted other potential breeding islands with native flora, and a new colony has been established on one of them, Nonsuch Island.

# Andean Flamingo

*Phoenicoparrus andinus*

*The rarest of the world's five species of flamingos, the Andean flamingo lives in a few remote high mountain lakes of the Andes Mountains. Its survival is threatened by the continuing exploitation and deterioration of its habitat.*

The Andean flamingo belongs to one of the oldest of all bird families, which originated over 50 million years ago. Today they are found on the puna—a high, cold, dry plateau in the Andes Mountains, usually at heights of between 7,500 and 14,750 feet (2,300 and 4,500 m). They live in lakes, where they wade in water 10 times as salty as the sea.

Although the lakes appear to be inhospitable, they are productive habitats, containing huge concentrations of diatoms, or microscopic single-cell algae (plants that have no true stems, roots, and leaves) on which the flamingos feed. The bizarre-looking bills of Andean flamingos are specially adapted for feeding in shallow water. The birds dunk their heads in the water, holding the bill upside down. The bill contains rows of comblike structures with which the birds sieve out the tiny food items by pumping water through the bill with a pistonlike action of the large tongue.

## Multiple Threats

Only one species of flamingo, the greater flamingo, is not considered threatened. The other four, even with a combined population of several million birds, are considered at risk from hunting, because of a long breeding cycle, and because there are fewer than 30 major breeding sites in the world. The situation for the Andean flamingo is particularly serious: It has the smallest population, which showed a serious decline—equal to 24 percent—in the 15 years from the mid-1980s. Breeding success is consistently low; and since the adults are long-lived (up to 50 years), numbers are unlikely to recover for many years.

The species nests at only 10 or so major colonies; and despite their remoteness, the breeding sites are coming under increasing pressure. Away from the protected colonies the flamingos are still regularly hunted (on a small scale) for their meat, feathers, and fat, which is used in traditional medicine and considered to be a cure for tuberculosis in some parts of the Andes. Most of the birds killed are juveniles.

A more serious threat is posed by the removal of eggs by local people, especially if they are sold in quantity rather than being used for personal consumption. The problem was especially acute during the 1950s to the early 1980s, when many eggs were taken from nests each year.

Both an increase in mining activities near breeding colonies and the towns that service the mining developments pose major threats to the flamingo's habitat. Along with the problem of water pollution, increased disturbance at the colonies from human activity can cause breeding failure. The diversion of streams for mining operations and other uses or changes in weather also result in fluctuating water levels. Such factors can cause droughts and consequently a lack of food or destruction of nests by flooding.

Surveys of the high-altitude salt and alkaline lakes of the Andes have revealed the species' status and population trends and located new colonies. A priority in the future is to maintain habitat, halt deterioration, and prevent hunting and egg-collecting by protecting more breeding sites. Four sites currently receive official protection to some degree.

*The Andean flamingo is endangered for many reasons, but low breeding success is a critical factor.*

## DATA PANEL

**Andean flamingo**

*Phoenicoparrus andinus*

**Family:** Phoenicopteridae

**World population:** Fewer than 34,000 birds

**Distribution:** The high Andean plateaus of Peru, Argentina, Bolivia, and Chile

**Habitat:** High mountain alkaline and salt lakes

**Size:** Length: 39–42 in (99–110 cm)

**Form:** Large waterbird with long neck and long legs. Downward-bent bill, pale yellow at the base, black on the downcurved portion. Plumage pale pink with bright upperparts and deep wine-red tinge to head, neck, upper breast, and wing coverts (small feathers covering the base of the flight feathers). Primary flight feathers of wingtips form a large black triangular patch when the wings are closed. Young birds are gray with heavily streaked upperparts

**Diet:** Diatoms (microscopic single-cell algae)

**Breeding:** Breeds in large social colonies of birds (including other species). Female lays 1 white egg in shallow pit atop a nest of mud. Incubation period about 4 weeks; chicks have pale-gray down and are at first fed on a milklike secretion from the adults' upper digestive tract; they fledge at 10–12 weeks; acquire adult plumage at 3 years

**Related endangered species:** Chilean flamingo (*Phoenicopterus chilensis*) NT; lesser flamingo (*P. minor*) NT; puna flamingo (*Phoenicoparrus jamesi*) NT

**Status:** IUCN VU

PERU
BRAZIL
BOLIVIA
PARAGUAY
CHILE
ARGENTINA
URUGUAY

# Northern Bald Ibis

## *Geronticus eremita*

*With its red face and long, downcurved, red bill framed by a scruffy ruff of black feathers, the northern bald ibis has an odd charm of its own. It is one of the world's rarest birds, with a very small range and population.*

The northern bald ibis was once widespread and abundant, but it is now extremely localized. Its representation in hieroglyphics dating back 5,000 years shows that it was revered as a holy bird in ancient Egypt. It bred in many places in North Africa and the Near and Middle East and until the 17th century in the mountains of Germany, Austria, Switzerland, and the former Yugoslavia. At the beginning of the 20th century the bird was rediscovered in North Africa and the Middle East to Western science. It looked very like the bird in a 16th-century Swiss drawing, but experts did not believe such an exotic species could ever have lived in Europe until a semifossilized specimen that was definitely a northern bald ibis was found there.

### Decline and Persecution

The reasons for the species' decline are not known for certain. From the Middle Ages onward it was hunted for food, which may have contributed to its eventual extinction in Europe. Other factors probably included the conversion of the mountain meadows where it fed into farmland and possibly a cooling of the climate.

Following its scientific discovery, the northern bald ibis faced increased persecution as museum collectors raced to secure specimens of this rare, semimythical bird. Aided by local hunters, they wiped out whole colonies, including, by the 1930s, most of the remaining Algerian colonies and all those in Syria. The bird also faced increasing threats from the conversion of its habitat to farmland, the rising use of pesticides, and frequent droughts. By the mid-20th century the world breeding population had declined to one colony in Turkey, one in Algeria, and a few in Morocco.

### Turkey

The Turkish bald ibis colony at the town of Birecik on the Euphrates River survived only because local people believed that the bird was a symbol of fertility and that it served as a guide to pilgrims to

---

## DATA PANEL

**Northern bald ibis**

*Geronticus eremita*

**Family:** Threskiornithidae

**World population:** About 300 birds

**Distribution:** In Morocco breeds only at Sous-Massa National Park and nearby Tamri; captive-bred, released colony breeds at Birecik in Turkey

**Habitat:** Arid to semiarid, sparsely vegetated steppes on plains and rocky plateaus; cultivated fields and pastures. Wild birds breed on cliff ledges by sea

**Size:** Length: 27.5–31.5 in (70–80 cm); wingspan: 4.1–4.4 ft (1.3–1.4 m); male usually larger. Weight unknown

**Form:** Large, dark, storklike bird; iridescent black plumage shows bronze-green, copper, blue, purple, and violet gloss in sunlight; naked red face and crown; long, narrow feathers project from nape to form wispy ruff; long, red downcurved bill and relatively short reddish legs; broad wings show 3–4 separated primary feathers at tips in flight

**Diet:** Mainly grasshoppers, locusts, beetles, and small lizards; also woodlice, spiders, snails, scorpions, small fish, frogs, and tadpoles; occasionally nestling birds and small mammals; berries, young shoots, and other plant matter

**Breeding:** Breeds in colonies of 3–40 pairs; nest is loose platform of branches lined with grass, straw, and other material, including paper; female lays 2–4 brown-spotted, bluish-white eggs; incubation period lasts 3–4 weeks. Chicks fledge in 6–7 weeks

**Related endangered species:** Southern bald ibis (*Geronticus calvus*) VU; dwarf olive ibis (*Bostrychia bocagei*) CR; white-shouldered ibis (*Pseudibis davisoni*) CR; giant ibis (*P. gigantea*) CR; Asian crested ibis (*Nipponia nippon*) EN

**Status:** IUCN CR

MOROCCO

Tamri

Sous-Massa National Park

ALGERIA

Mecca. They held an annual festival to celebrate its return each February from winter quarters in Sudan and southern Arabia. However, when Birecik grew, the newcomers did not share the local people's reverence for the ibis, and the festival was not held after 1958. As the town expanded, the bird's nesting grounds were absorbed. From an estimated 3,000 pairs in 1890 the population was reduced to 530 pairs by 1953 and 23 pairs by 1973.

The chief causes of this catastrophic decline were the use of pesticides in the surrounding habitat and the increasing human disturbance at the colonies. In 1977 a colony of captive-bred birds was created by conservationists 1.3 miles (2 km) north of Birecik, with the aim of encouraging the wild birds breeding in the town to relocate to this site. However, most of the released birds failed to integrate with the wild population, which meant that they did not migrate (the young have to learn to migrate from their parents) and so perished during the winter.

Lack of food, problems capturing wild birds, the late release of juveniles, plus the failure of the Turkish government to ban the use of pesticides resulted in a steeper decline in the population. By spring 1989 only three wild birds returned from their winter quarters, and two later died in accidents. The species was effectively extinct in the wild at Birecik, although there are now about 100 non-migratory birds there.

## Morocco

The ibis has fared better at its two surviving sites in Morocco, but has still faced severe problems, especially hunting, pesticide poisoning, and habitat loss as a result of dam building. In 1991 the Sous-Massa National Park was established specifically to protect the breeding and feeding areas of the ibis. In 1994 the Moroccan breeding population was estimated to be 300. In May 1996, 40 birds died mysteriously, possibly from botulism or unknown toxins. By 1998 numbers had declined to about 200 birds, but there has been a slight increase since then.

**The northern bald ibis** *uses its long, downcurved bill to extract prey. It probes into crevices, among tufts of vegetation, in sand, soft soil, and under stones.*

# White-headed Duck

## Oxyura leucocephala

*Long-term population declines for the white-headed duck have recently intensified as a result of habitat loss at a key wintering site. Threats of competition from the introduced North American ruddy duck have also been a problem.*

The white-headed duck probably had a global population of over 100,000 in the early 20th century; in the 1930s an estimated 50,000 wintered on the Caspian Sea. However, by 1991 the population was estimated at a mere 19,000 ducks. This reduction in numbers was matched by a large decline in breeding range. Over the last 100 years the white-headed duck has become extinct as a breeding bird in Albania, Azerbaijan, Corsica, Hungary, Italy, Israel, Morocco, and the former Yugoslavia. Despite the historical declines, however, there was some optimism in 1991, since the population was thought to be relatively stable.

After 1991 that optimism faded. Numbers plummeted in the following decade to fewer than 10,000 birds. The decline was most severe at what was the most important wintering site, Burdur Gölü in Turkey. In 1991 about 10,900 birds wintered there, but in 1996 only 1,270 were recorded. Obviously, some of the birds have simply scattered to other wetland sites, and wintering numbers have increased elsewhere in the eastern Mediterranean region. They include the doubling of the population at Lake Vistonis, Greece, with other large increases in Bulgaria and Romania. However, the counts do not compensate for the very large declines at Burdur Gölü.

### Reasons for the Decline

The large historical declines are mostly the result of extensive drainage of wetlands, particularly in the former Soviet Union and Spain. Over 50 percent of breeding habitat was destroyed during the 20th century, and the remaining sites are especially vulnerable to eutrophication (overenrichment by nutrients, particularly nitrates and phosphates) and pollution. The range of threats includes industrial, domestic, and agricultural pollution, sedimentation, and water extraction, as seen at Burdur Gölü and the Sultan marshes in central southern Turkey. At Lake Vistonis drowning in fishing nets is a severe threat. Dead birds have also been found in nets at sites in Spain and Turkey.

## DATA PANEL

**White-headed duck**

*Oxyura leucocephala*

**Family:** Anatidae

**World population:** 7,900–13,100 birds

**Distribution:** Algeria, Spain, and Tunisia; most birds breed in Russia and Kazakhstan, smaller populations in Afghanistan, Iran, Mongolia, Turkey, and Uzbekistan. Eastern populations occur and winter in the eastern Mediterranean, Middle East, Central Asia, and the Indian subcontinent

**Habitat:** Breeds on small, shallow, freshwater or brackish lakes with dense vegetation at fringes. Winter lakes are larger and deeper with little emergent vegetation. In Spain and Tunisia, artificial lagoons and reservoirs

**Size:** Length: 17–19 in (43–48 cm); wingspan: 24.5–27.5 in (62–70 cm). Weight: male 25–32 oz (720–900 g); female 19–28 oz (550–800 g)

**Form:** Chestnut-brown diving duck; long tail, often cocked vertically. Male has white head, black cap, and blue bill, swollen at base. Female has pale face with dark cap, and cheek stripe; blackish, less swollen bill

**Diet:** In Spain benthic (bottom-dwelling) chironomid larvae and pupae; wintering birds in Greece feed primarily on polychaete worms

**Breeding:** Polygamous (has more than 1 mate); nests in dense reedbeds, often on top of old coot nests. Timing is variable, with 4–9 eggs laid April and early July. Incubation takes 3–3.5 weeks, fledging 8–9 weeks

**Related endangered species:** Twenty-one others, including pink-headed duck *(Rhodonessa caryophyllacea)* CR

**Status:** IUCN EN

*White-headed duck populations have suffered through widespread habitat loss and cross-breeding with the ruddy duck.*

## Ruddy Duck Danger

While a major problem for the white-headed duck is habitat loss, western European populations are also threatened by hybridization and competition with the North American ruddy duck. The ruddy duck was introduced to Britain in the 1950s and is now spreading across western and into central Europe. It has been seen in 20 countries, and breeding has been recorded in six. This introduced species cross-breeds readily with the white-headed duck, and hybrids are fully fertile; second-generation birds have also been collected in Spain. The real concern is that the ruddy duck will spread eastward into the core of the white-headed duck's range. If it spreads into Algeria, Turkey, or Russia, the size of the wetlands—which are infrequently monitored—will make control impossible.

## Conservation Measures

Measures are being taken to control the ruddy duck in France, Portugal, Spain, and the Netherlands. In Britain a program to eradicate ruddy ducks was very successful, reducing numbers from 4,400 in 2005 to just 200 in 2010. The Spanish control program is one element of a highly effective conservation strategy that was started in 1979. Since then a reduction in illegal hunting, the regeneration of natural vegetation, the release of captive-bred birds into the wild, and from 1989 shooting of ruddy ducks and hybrids has led to a dramatic population recovery.

The challenge is to replicate the success of the Spanish program for more easterly populations. The effective protection of wetlands in Russia and Kazahkstan is a high priority. Without such protection it is almost certain that the white-headed duck will continue its dramatic decline.

# Nene

## Branta sandvicensis

*Unique to the Hawaiian Islands, the nene was driven to the verge of extinction by the destruction of its wild habitats and the introduction of predators. By 1950 there were only about 30 left on Hawaii, but captive breeding has helped, and the nene may soon be thriving again in the wild.*

The volcanic Hawaiian Islands were once home to a unique variety of birdlife, including at least 11 species of waterfowl found nowhere else in the world. Perfectly adapted for life on the islands, where the only native predators were birds of prey, several of the geese and ducks were flightless. When the Polynesians arrived about 1,600 years ago, the birds were sitting targets, and most are now extinct. Only three of the 11 now survive, including the one big goose that was able to fly: the nene.

Also known as the Hawaiian goose, the nene is named for its high, nasal, two-note "né-né" call. Although it can fly, it has quite short wings—too short for a long migration. Fossil evidence shows that it once occurred throughout the Hawaiian chain. To make up for its short wings, it has unusually long legs, with big, strong feet. Since there is little wetland on the islands, it has little webbing between its toes, which are padded

to help it scramble over the rocky lava flows that spill down the flanks of the island volcanoes.

Drinking water is hard to find on the islands, so the essentially vegetarian nene seeks out moisture-rich plants for food. In season it plucks berries from the bushes between the lava flows, making the most of its long legs to reach up into the foliage.

### Hunted Out

The Polynesian settlers brought their pigs, dogs, and—accidentally—the Polynesian rat. They all played havoc with the ground-nesting nene. People also burned off the lowland scrub to create pasture, destroying vital cover for the breeding geese. Yet the nene survived, and there were at least 25,000 of them at the end of the 18th century, when Europeans reached the islands. The new settlers introduced more killers: black rats, cats, and in 1883 the small Indian mongoose. They also had guns; between them human hunters and predators eliminated the nene from the lowlands.

## DATA PANEL

**Nene (Hawaiian goose)**

**Branta sandvicensis**

**Family:** Anatidae

**World population:** About 1,200

**Distribution:** Originally throughout Hawaiian archipelago, but reduced to a few wild birds on Hawaii by 1950; following reintroductions, it now lives wild on Hawaii, Maui, and Kauai

**Habitat:** Grassy shrublands and sparsely

vegetated, semiarid basalt lava flows on volcanic slopes; lowland pasture on Kauai

**Size:** Length: 25–27 in (63–69 cm). Weight: 2.9–6.6 lb (1.3–3 kg)

**Form:** Small, erect goose with short wings, long legs, and strong feet with reduced webbing. Black bill, face, and crown; golden-buff neck with unique dark furrows; upperparts and breast sepia brown with pattern of dark gray and white; white belly

**Diet:** Moist vegetation such as grass, leaves and berries, and seeds

**Breeding:** Birds pair for life and breed in November–January; 3–5 white eggs laid in a nest scrape and incubated by female for about 4 weeks while male stands guard; young fledge in about 10–12 weeks

**Related endangered species:** In Hawaiian Islands, Laysan duck (*Anas laysanensis*) CR; Hawaiian duck (*A. wyvilliana*) EN. Other threatened geese include the lesser white-fronted goose (*Anser erythropus*) VU and the red-breasted goose (*Branta ruficollis*) EN

**Status:** IUCN VU

By 1907, when hunting was banned, the nene was probably found only on Hawaii itself. It had retreated into the volcanic uplands where mongoose and cats were scarce, yet while the near-barren slopes provided enough food for bare survival, the extra nutrients needed for producing eggs and feeding young were often lacking. In poor seasons many adult geese failed to breed, and the young birds that did hatch often died from malnutrition. By 1949 there were perhaps only 30 left.

## Rescue

The recovery of the nene is almost entirely due to captive breeding. In 1950 three birds were acquired by what is now the Wildfowl and Wetlands Trust at Slimbridge, England, and they became the foundation of a captive-bred flock of 2,000 or so. Meanwhile, the birds were also being bred in captivity on Hawaii. In 1960 a reintroduction program started, and since then over 2,300 geese have been released into protected areas on Hawaii and the neighboring island of Maui.

On Hawaii and Maui the reintroduced nene live in the uplands, where they still suffer from bad weather and malnutrition. On Hawaii the nene population of about 350 has to be boosted by new introductions and given extra food. On Maui the population of just over 200 is relatively stable.

Birds have been introduced to the more distant island of Kauai. There the population has increased to around 620. There is no mongoose predation, allowing the nene to live in the coastal lowlands, where they enjoy a better diet.

Conservation bodies aim to establish large, predator-free reserves in lowland areas. The elimination of poaching and reduction of roadkills are also planned. If coupled with translocations of stock between islands to minimize inbreeding, the nene may be on track for a full recovery.

*The nene is a relative of the Canada goose. It evolved on the Hawaiian Islands into a species with shortened wings and half-webbed feet.*

# Philippine Eagle

## *Pithecophaga jefferyi*

*One of the rarest of the world's birds of prey, the Philippine eagle is in a precarious situation. Its small and rapidly declining population is threatened by forest destruction and fragmentation.*

The Philippine eagle is a flagship species for wildlife conservation on four of the Philippine group of islands. Predictions of its imminent extinction have been made since the 1960s, but the species hangs on in the face of immense odds. Conservationists believe that most of the population is equally distributed between the large islands of Luzon and Mindanao (an estimated 105 pairs), while the smaller islands of Samar and Leyte house only an estimated eight pairs between them. However, these figures are based mostly on forest-cover data, and more precise information on numbers is not available.

The Philippine eagle is a huge and powerful predator. It waits on a perch high in the rain forest canopy, looking and listening for the slightest movement or sound that betrays prey beneath. Its relatively short, rounded wings and long tail equip it for weaving deftly among the trees. It often begins a hunt at the top of a hillside and works its way down; it starts the process again when it reaches the bottom.

The Philippine eagle was once known as the monkey-eating eagle. Although it eats various species of monkey, it more often feeds on two cat-sized mammals: the flying lemur and the palm civet. It is likely that the eagle is also an opportunistic hunter, taking different prey according to its availability and abundance. Each pair hunts in a large territory of about 23 to 38 square miles (60 to 100 sq. km). As in other eagle species, the pairs mate for life.

## Lost Forest

As with so many other species, the main threat facing the Philippine eagle is the relentless destruction of its habitat. Every year some of the remaining primary forest on the islands is felled for timber: The great

## DATA PANEL

### Philippine eagle (monkey-eating eagle)

*Pithecophaga jefferyi*

**Family:** Accipitridae

**World population:** 250–500 birds; possibly only 226 mature adults

**Distribution:** Philippine islands of Luzon, Leyte, Mindanao, and Samar

**Habitat:** Primary dipterocarp (hardwood) rain forest on steep slopes; sometimes lives among secondary growth and gallery forest along riverbanks and floodplains. Occurs from the lowlands to 5,900 ft (1,800 m)

**Size:** Length: 34–40 in (86–102 cm); wingspan: about 6.5 ft (2 m). Weight: 10.3–17.6 lb (4.7–8 kg)

**Form:** Huge eagle with large, arched, powerfully hooked blue bill. Dark area around eyes (which have pale blue-gray irises) contrasts with buff crown and nape; long, spiky, black-streaked feathers form scruffy crest; cheeks, throat, underparts, and underwings white; upperparts and upperwings dark brown; legs and feet yellow

**Diet:** Tree-dwelling mammals such as flying lemurs, palm civets, monkeys, and flying squirrels; also tree-dwelling birds, including hornbills, owls, and hawks; bats, monitor lizards, and snakes

**Breeding:** Female lays 1 white egg in huge stick nest high in canopy of tall tree, usually on an epiphytic fern (one that grows on another plant). Both sexes incubate for about 9 weeks; eaglet fledges after about 5 months; remains dependent on parents for another year or more

**Related endangered species:** New Guinea eagle (*Harpyopsis novaeguineae*) VU; harpy eagle (*Harpia harpyja*) NT

**Status:** IUCN CR

dipterocarp (tall hardwood) trees growing there are a major source of tropical timber for the rest of the world. When the loggers leave, settlers who practice "slash-and-burn" cultivation frequently move in. Slash-and-burn agriculture produces poor-quality, weed-infested grassland with bamboo or other scrub in place of a rich forest and is of little value to the eagles.

With the increasing numbers of people moving into the forests, it is probable that only 3,560 square miles (9,220 sq. km) of forest remain. Even national parks are severely affected; in Mount Apo National Park, for instance, over 50 percent of the original forest has disappeared.

Other threats facing the Philippine eagle include hunting by local people for food or trophies and, until recently, the capture of young for sale to zoos and the cage-bird trade. Plans for mining operations have also caused concern. There is evidence that the eagles accumulate pesticides from their prey in their body, a factor that is likely to affect their breeding success—a serious problem in a species that produces only one young every two years, at most.

## Last Hope

Over the past 30 to 40 years various conservation initiatives have been launched to assure the future of the Philippine eagle. Plans include protective legislation, surveys, captive breeding, public awareness programs, and a sustainable agriculture project designed to improve conditions for both eagles and local people. However, relatively little is still known of the bird's ecology, and the work has been hampered at intervals by natural disasters and serious political unrest, as well as by the difficult nature of the remote habitats the eagle favors.

**The Philippine eagle** *perches high up in the rain forest canopy, watching for prey. Plans for its conservation include a campaign to foster national pride in the bird. If that is successful, the eagle may yet avoid extinction in the wild.*

# Spanish Imperial Eagle

## *Aquila adalberti*

*One of the world's rarest birds of prey, the Spanish imperial eagle was thought to be in recovery in the early 1980s, but recently numbers have declined again. Like many other birds of prey, it has come into increasing conflict with the demands of people and is now seriously threatened.*

At the beginning of the 20th century the Spanish imperial eagle was still relatively common and widespread. It could be found over most of Spain in areas of dry, uncultivated habitat. It also bred in Portugal and Morocco.

Today the species has disappeared from much of its range as a result of the loss and fragmentation of its forest habitat. By the 1960s the Spanish imperial eagle was almost extinct, with only 30 pairs recorded. Conservationists tried a new rescue technique. First,

they located nests with three or four eaglets. The last chicks to hatch often die as a result of the so-called Cain and Abel conflict. The "conflict" describes the tendency of the stronger nestlings to kill their younger siblings—as Cain killed his brother Abel in the biblical story. Sometimes the weaker siblings starve, since they are not strong enough to compete for the food brought by their parents.

Rescued eaglets were then put into nests with only a single chick. The number of surviving fledglings increased by up to 43 percent. From the early 1980s the species started to recover, and an average of five new breeding pairs appeared each year until 1994. The population then declined from 148 pairs in 1994 to 131 pairs in 1998, but by 2005 the trend had reversed again to lift the population to approximately 200 pairs.

### Threats to Survival

Spanish imperial eagles need large areas of open forest with scattered trees or clumps of woodland for nesting and rough grassland or open ground for hunting. The birds avoid areas that have been irrigated for crops and site their nests well away from settlements, roads, and other developments. Wild places are increasingly difficult to find as more people move into undeveloped areas. The eagles are sensitive to disturbance, which can affect their breeding success.

Another major factor affecting the eagle's success is the availability

## DATA PANEL

**Spanish imperial eagle (Adalbert's eagle)**

*Aquila adalberti*

**Family:** Accipitridae

**World population:** About 400 birds

**Distribution:** Breeds in central and southwestern Spain, in the Sierras of Guadarrama and Gredos, plains of Tajo and Tiétar Rivers, the central hills of Extremadura, Montes de Toledo, the Alcudia Valley, Sierra Morena, and the Guadalquivir marshes; also Salamanca and Málaga; eastern Portugal

**Habitat:** Open, wooded areas away from irrigated and cultivated farmland; high mountain slopes; hills and plains; sand dunes and alluvial plains

**Size:** Length: 29.5–33 in (75–84 cm); wingspan: 6–8 ft (1.8–2.4 m). Weight: 5.5–7.7 lb (2.5–3.5 kg)

**Form:** Huge bird of prey with dark plumage. Brown-black coloration with white "shoulders," pale-golden nape,

and pale-gray base to upper tail. Juveniles have rust-colored plumage that fades to pale buff; dark flight feathers; white fringes to wing coverts (feathers covering the flight feathers)

**Diet:** Mainly mammals, especially rabbits; also pigeons, waterbirds, gamebirds, and members of the crow family; occasionally snakes and lizards. Also dead cows and other grazing mammals

**Breeding:** Large stick nest built in tree; female usually lays 2–4 brown-blotched whitish eggs that are incubated for about 6 weeks; young fledge in about 10 weeks

**Related endangered species:** Imperial eagle (*Aquila heliaca*) VU; greater spotted eagle (*A. clanga*) VU

**Status:** IUCN VU

FRANCE
SPAIN
PORTUGAL
ALGERIA

of rabbits. Rabbits usually form more than half of the eagle's total prey—in some places as much as 70 percent. However, the viral disease myxomatosis, deliberately introduced to control rabbit populations in 1957, was very effective. In a few areas eagles switched to hunting alternative prey. It is likely that many pairs were forced to stop breeding due to the shortage of rabbits. Another viral disease— hemorrhagic pneumonia—has added to the drop in rabbit numbers: in some areas by 80 percent.

Deliberate and accidental poisoning of the eagles is another cause of the bird's decline, especially in hunting preserves where game animals are commercially exploited. Carcasses baited with powerful poisons are now a significant cause of death. Such traps kill other species, too, including domestic dogs. Between 1989 and 1999 at least 57 Spanish imperial eagles died from poisoning—probably more than by any other means.

The eagles are also vulnerable to electrocution by power cables. Inexperienced juveniles are most at risk, especially when their plumage is wet. There are more deaths when power lines are sited away from roads and in areas where there are large numbers of rabbits.

## Conservation Plans

Although 60 percent of the breeding population lives in 20 protected areas, the species still needs urgent help. A coordinated conservation plan is being implemented. Priorities include annual censuses of the breeding population, protecting nesting areas, increasing the rabbit population, working toward the elimination of poisoning, and surveying and modifying power lines to prevent electrocution.

**The Spanish imperial eagle** *is a huge bird of prey with a wingspan of between 6 and 8 feet (1.8 and 2.4 m).*

EX

EW

CR

EN

VU

NT

LC

O

# Red Kite

## *Milvus milvus*

*After an apparently relentless decline stretching over three or four centuries, the red kite is staging a comeback in the northwest of its range, thanks largely to the efforts of conservationists.*

**B**ig, beautiful, and almost balletic in its mastery of the sky, the red kite is one of the world's most spectacular raptors. Instantly identifiable by its rich, chestnut plumage and forked tail, it flies with a buoyant, airy grace that seems to defy gravity. It flourishes particularly in open, half-wild country with scattered woodlands, where it can locate food from the air and find plenty of trees for roosting.

At one time the kite was a common sight over much of Europe, even in major cities, for although it is a hunter, its real talent lies in scavenging easy meals from carcasses and refuse dumps. Back in the 16th century there were rich pickings to be had from every back alley, and the practice of allowing farm animals to roam over unfenced land ensured a steady supply of carrion. Yet by the end of the Middle Ages it was on the brink of a long, slow decline in numbers.

It disappeared from the cities first. Improved hygiene eliminated edible garbage from the streets. Like many other raptors, the kite was declared vermin, but its leisurely flight style made it an easier target than most. As guns became widespread during the 18th and 19th centuries, the red kite was gradually shot out of the skies. Others were trapped or poisoned; since they feed from carcasses, they can fall victim to poisoned bait laid out for other animals.

At the same time, agriculture was becoming more scientific, and farmers were abandoning the old ways in favor of more intensive systems. In the lowlands the supply of carrion began to dry up; and when chemical pesticides came into common use, live prey began to disappear too. Gradually, the kites retreated to the mountains and moors, where they could still find food and secure nesting sites.

In many places they are still declining. In eastern Europe the intensification of agriculture following land privatization has reduced their habitat. Yet the most endangered population was the distinctive, smaller race that once flourished on the Cape Verde Islands, off West Africa. Its numbers began to dwindle in the 1960s, partly because of the virtual destruction of the natural ecosystem on many of the islands and partly because the red kites were interbreeding with similar black kites. By the year 2000 the Cape Verde population was effectively extinct.

### Welsh Revival

In sharp contrast, conservation efforts in northwestern Europe have led to a kite revival. In Britain, for example, a tiny relict population of red kites managed to survive in the mountains of central Wales, where they were able to exploit a steady supply of rabbit and sheep carcasses. Yet in 1903, when conservation began, they were on the edge of extinction, with only

12 birds left. Since then intensive research, better protection, supplementary feeding, and the cooperation of local farmers have gradually enabled the Welsh kites to bounce back. By 2008 there were 750–800 pairs in Wales. Meanwhile, kites from southern Sweden and northern Spain were introduced into hill country in several areas of England and Scotland, with dramatic success—there were up to 800 pairs in England and Scotland by 2008.

The Welsh experience shows that the red kite is a survivor; given the right conditions, it can breed its way back from near-oblivion. Other countries in northwestern Europe are reporting similar increases, which partly offset the losses in other parts of its range. Yet ultimately its future may depend on the survival of another endangered species: the organic farmer, whose pesticide-free fields nurture the wild plants and insects that form the basis of the ecosystem on which the bird depends.

**The red kite** *includes carrion in its diet and is susceptible to both deliberate and accidental poisoning of carcasses.*

## DATA PANEL

Red kite

*Milvus milvus*

**Family:** Accipitridae

**World population:** 21,000–25,500 breeding pairs

**Distribution:** From western Russia west to Wales, Spain, and the Cape Verde Islands; from southern Sweden south to Sicily and northwestern Morocco

**Habitat:** Mixed country, often hilly, with woodland for nesting and meadows, lakes, and rivers

**Size:** Length: 24–26 in (60–66 cm); wingspan: 5.7–6.4 ft (1.8–2 m). Weight: 1.8–2.9 lb (0.8–1.3 kg); females larger than males

**Form:** Sleek, graceful bird of prey with long wings, long, deeply forked tail, and feathered legs. Gray-white head; red-brown upperparts with black wingtips; rich chestnut underparts and tail; large, pale patches on undersides of outer wings. Bright yellow eyes, black-tipped yellow bill, yellow feet, black talons

**Diet:** Birds, small mammals, fish, large insects, earthworms, carrion, and scraps

**Breeding:** In March–May 2–4 eggs are laid in a nest of sticks and mud, often incorporating scraps of paper, plastic, or cloth, high in a tall tree or, rarely, on a cliff. The nest is often built on top of an abandoned buzzard's or crow's nest, and the same site is often reused every year for decades. The female incubates the eggs for 31–32 days, and the chicks fledge after 48–60 days

**Related endangered species:** Many birds of prey in the family Accipitridae

**Status:** IUCN NT

# California Condor

*Gymnogyps californianus*

*The California condor has already been extinct in the wild once, and only the reintroduction and management of captive-bred birds is preventing its disappearance for a second time.*

There is evidence that the massive California condor once lived across a wide range in the United States. Since 1937, however, it has been confined to California in the nation's southwestern corner. This decline in range was matched throughout the 20th century by a continuing fall in numbers, driven by human activity and in particular by the widespread availability of firearms. Many birds were shot and killed; others suffered indirectly by ingesting lead from the carcasses of animals that had been shot and abandoned, leading to death by lead poisoning. By 1987 the California condor's situation had become so critical that the last six wild individuals were captured for inclusion in a captive-breeding program. The magnificent creature had formally become extinct in the wild.

At that time there were already 16 birds in captivity, so the total population stood at only 22 birds. Since then a large-scale, integrated breeding and reintroduction program has been in operation. It has had notable success; by November 2010 the total population had increased to 381 birds, of which 192 were living in the wild. The other 189 are still in captivity, divided between breeding facilities managed respectively by the Peregrine Fund at the World Center for Birds of Prey, by the Los Angeles Zoo, by the San Diego Wild Animal Park, and by the Oregon Zoo. The remaining birds have been reintroduced back to the wild at five separate sites in California, Arizona, and Baja, Mexico. There are now 100 wild birds in California, at several locations. Another 73 wild individuals are in Arizona, and in 2007 a California condor laid an egg in Mexico for the first time since at least the 1930s.

## Problems in the Wild

Unfortunately, the recovery program is all that is stopping the species from becoming extinct in the wild for a second time, since the released birds still depend on the ongoing work of the program for their continued survival. None of the birds has yet reached reproductive maturity, and in addition they all currently rely on food provided by the program.

## DATA PANEL

**California condor**

*Gymnogyps californianus*

**Family:** Cathartidae

**World population:** At the end of 2010 the total wild population was 173

**Distribution:** Birds have been reintroduced in 5 areas, 3 in California and 2 in northern Arizona

**Habitat:** Rocky, open-country scrubland terrain, coniferous forests, and oak savanna

**Size:** Length: 46–54 in (117–134 cm); wingspan: 9 ft (2.7 m). Weight: 17.6–31 lb (8–14 kg)

**Form:** Huge, unmistakable raptor (bird of prey). Mostly black with white wing-linings and silvery panel on upper secondaries. The head is naked and orange-red. Immatures have black heads and dark mottling on the underwing. When soaring, the wings are held horizontally, with the outermost wing feathers curled up

**Diet:** Scavenges the carcasses of large mammals, although the reintroduced birds currently rely on food provided by the recovery program

**Breeding:** Nest sites are located in cavities in cliffs, on rocky outcrops, or in large trees. Clearly adapted for very low reproductive output

**Related endangered species:** Andean condor *(Vultur gryphus)* LRnt

**Status:** IUCN CR

Nor have they found it easy to readapt to conditions in the wild. The first birds to be released suffered from behavioral difficulties and tended to collide with powerlines. This had not previously been a problem with the species and such accidents may have been caused by the captive-bred birds getting used to human-made structures. Following the deaths of a number of newly released individuals, a program of "aversion training" was introduced that has involved conditioning the birds to avoid powerlines and all contact with humans. The first of the conditioned birds was released in 1995, and so far the training appears to have been successful.

Other grounds for optimism include the fact that at some of the release sites the birds are increasingly finding food of their own. In addition, at certain times of the year they are now ranging up to 250 miles (400 km) away from the sites. In the meantime the provision of clean carcasses does have the added benefit of avoiding any possibility of lead poisoning.

## Ambitious Targets

The current conservation action plan for the species has set several ambitious targets. A long-term goal is to establish two self-sustaining populations of at least 150 individuals each, including 15 breeding pairs. For this

goal to be realized, all aspects of the current program must be continued. One key factor is the maintenance of the birds' habitat. Another is the implementation of information and education programs, which will raise awareness of the California condor's plight. Without such efforts persecution may begin again as the birds become increasingly widespread.

**California condors**
*came close to extinction in the late 1980s, when the total population of the species was reduced to just 22 birds.*

# Mauritius Kestrel

## *Falco punctatus*

*Reduced to a population of just four wild birds by 1974, the Mauritius kestrel has clawed its way back from the edge of extinction to become a spectacular success story.*

The island of Mauritius in the Indian Ocean will always be notorious as the former home of the dodo: the universal symbol of extinction. Until recently the Mauritius kestrel seemed bound to suffer the same fate since its numbers had reached a point from which recovery seemed impossible.

The Mauritius kestrel hunts like a short-winged sparrowhawk. Its relatively short wings give it the maneuverability to pursue prey beneath the canopy of dense evergreen forest that once covered much of the island. It usually hunts from a perch, moving swiftly and swerving through the branches to snatch prey (songbirds, dragonflies, or lizards) from the air or the trees. Among its favorite targets are the iridescent green geckos found only on Mauritius; the kestrel is expert at locating them as they bask, immobile in the sun. Occasionally, it hovers to pinpoint prey in low vegetation, but its wings are not really adapted to the task. It is a bird of the forests. As the forests were felled to provide farmland for a growing population, the kestrel gradually disappeared.

### Relentless Decline

Mauritius kestrels have never been abundant. Each breeding pair occupies a large territory, and the entire island is no bigger than a large city. At most there were probably only 1,000 birds. By the 1970s rampant deforestation had eliminated most native forest cover, leaving only a few pockets of habitat in rocky gorges on the southwest of the island. The kestrels were also shot by farmers—who believed they stole poultry—and poisoned by pesticides. Their tree nesting sites were vulnerable to the egg-thieving nonnative macaque monkeys, as well as introduced cats, rats, and mongoose. It was a deadly combination, and by 1974 there were just four birds.

That season one pair nested in a tree in the usual way, but their nest was raided by monkeys. For some reason the other pair chose to nest in a hole in a sheer cliff. The choice of this unusual nesting site saved the species because the cliff face was monkey-proof. Three chicks fledged, and for the first time in years the Mauritius kestrel population increased. The young birds adopted the

**Mauritius kestrels** *are currently being studied to determine their genetic variation so that their genetic diversity can be maintained.*

## DATA PANEL

**Mauritius kestrel**

*Falco punctatus*

**Family:** Falconidae

**World population:** More than 800 birds

**Distribution:** Island of Mauritius in the southwestern Indian Ocean

**Habitat:** Primarily evergreen subtropical forest, but captive-bred birds released into the wild have colonized degraded secondary forest and scrub

**Size:** Length: 8–10 in (20–26 cm). Weight: male 6 oz (178 g); female 8 oz (231 g)

**Form:** Small and stocky, with long legs and tail; unusually short, rounded wings for a kestrel. Female bigger than male. Black-barred, chestnut-colored upperparts, black-flecked white underparts, black eye with typical dark falcon "moustache" below; yellow skin on legs and at base of bill. Juvenile has blue-gray facial skin

**Diet:** Lizards (mainly tree-climbing geckos), small birds, large insects, and introduced mice and shrews

**Breeding:** Naturally nests in tree cavities, but may now use cliff sites and nest boxes; lays 2–5 (usually 3) eggs in August–November; young hatch after 4 weeks

**Related endangered species:** Seychelles kestrel *(Falco araea)* VU; lesser kestrel *(F. naumanni)* VU

**Status:** IUCN VU

COMOROS

MADAGASCAR

MAURITIUS

Réunion (France)

---

cliff-nesting habit when they matured, and by 1976 they had boosted the population to 15 birds.

## Revival

Early attempts to breed Mauritius kestrels in captivity ended in failure. The first success came in 1984, and since then many birds have been bred in captivity both in Mauritius and at the World Center for Birds of Prey in Boise, Idaho. By 1993 there were 200 birds.

The object was always to reintroduce the birds to the wild. Released captive-bred birds initially had trouble establishing territories in areas where there were wild kestrels; only about 50 percent of birds released in prime habitat survived their first year.

It was assumed that Mauritius kestrels would not thrive in other types of terrain, but the captive-bred

birds have proved adaptable. Released into areas of degraded secondary forest, their survival rate after a year is about 80 percent. By the end of the 1999 to 2000 breeding season there were three subpopulations, including between 145 and 200 breeding pairs. At first the birds were sustained by supplementary feeding, nest-guarding, predator control, and other conservation measures. But since 1994 there have been no more reintroductions, and the kestrels have virtually been left to their own devices. By 2008 there were more than 800 individuals.

The Mauritius kestrel will never be quite safe: Its total population is so small that it will always be vulnerable to natural disasters such as tropical storms and infectious diseases. However, its story shows what can be done, given the will and a little luck.

# Whooping Crane

## *Grus americana*

*Intensive conservation efforts have pulled the whooping crane back from the brink of extinction. There is now hope that this rescue initiative is turning into a conservation success story.*

In the mid-19th century the population of whooping cranes numbered between 1,300 and 1,400 birds. By 1938 heavy hunting pressure, widespread habitat conversion, and general disturbance by people had reduced the population to just 14 adults. Such a large reduction in numbers was inevitably accompanied by a huge contraction in range, and many populations became extinct.

There is now only one self-sustaining wild population, breeding in the wet prairies of Wood Buffalo National Park in central Canada. This population of 266 birds includes 65 breeding pairs and has been increasing slowly at about 5 percent per year since 1966. The major hope for the species' continuing survival rests with the wild Canadian flock.

## Reintroduced Birds

A reintroduced population of about 41 exists in Florida, but numbers are maintained by the annual introduction of more birds from captivity. However, there are hopes that the Florida population will become self-sustaining, which is not the case for the reintroduced birds in Idaho. This was an experimental flock, cross-fostered by sandhill cranes, but the birds have not reproduced. An introduced flock migrates between Wisconsin and Florida.

## Current Problems

Hunting and large-scale habitat loss are no longer key threats to the populations. Currently the largest known cause of death or injury to fledglings is collision with powerlines. Since overall numbers are still low, predation by golden eagles is also believed to be highly significant, especially on migration routes.

Drought is thought to be a cause of the deterioration of some breeding habitats, but availability of habitat on breeding grounds is probably not a limiting factor for the near future. There are more important threats, such as those affecting the major wintering site, Aransas National Wildlife Refuge, Texas: the risk of oil and chemical pollution, and problems related to boat traffic, wave erosion, and dredging.

## DATA PANEL

**Whooping crane**

**Grus americana**

**Family:** Gruidae

**World population:** About 380 birds in the wild

**Distribution:** Wild population breeds in Wood Buffalo National Park, on the border of Northwest Territories and Alberta, Canada. Winters at Aransas National Wildlife Refuge, Texas. Flocks have been reintroduced to Florida and Idaho, with former nonmigratory and latter wintering south to New Mexico

**Habitat:** Breeds in prairie wetlands and winters in coastal brackish wetlands

**Size:** Length: 4.4 ft (1.3 m); wingspan: 7–8 ft (2–2.4 m). Weight: 16.5 lb (7.5 kg)

**Form:** Huge bird with large, horn-colored bill. Adults show black forehead, lores (area between eyes and base of bill), and "moustache," tipped red. Red crown and facial skin around bill. Black primary feathers visible in flight. Immatures whitish, with scattered brown feathers over wings and paler red-brown head and neck

**Diet:** In Canada snails, larval insects, leeches, frogs, minnows, small rodents, and berries; sometimes scavenges on dead ducks, marsh birds, or muskrats. During migration aquatic animals, plants roots, and waste grain in stubble fields. In Texas shellfish, snakes, acorns, small fish, and wild fruit

**Breeding:** Two eggs laid between late April and mid-May and incubated for about 1 month; usually only 1 fledges

**Related endangered species:** Include blue crane (*Grus paradisea*) VU; black-necked crane (*G. nigricollis*) VU; Siberian crane (*G. leucogeranus*) CR; wattled crane (*G. carunculatus*) VU

**Status:** IUCN EN

Wood Buffalo National Park

CANADA

UNITED STATES

Aransas National Wildlife Refuge

MEXICO

## Conservation Targets

Only an intensive conservation effort has prevented the whooping crane from disappearing into extinction. Its objectives have been to maintain one self-sustaining population and to increase the captive population for further releases of birds into the wild.

Captive birds are held at several locations in the United States, and at Calgary in Canada. In the special facilities whooping crane chicks are kept in isolation from humans. They are fed through a hole in the wall by an adult whooping crane glove puppet. Simulation of this kind is designed to make the birds' eventual introduction to the wild as successful as possible. Since the choice of migration routes, nesting locations, and wintering sites is learned rather than instinctive, the captive-breeding programs also focus on teaching birds to migrate by following light aircraft or vehicles on the ground.

The species is the subject of a transnational recovery plan, which has a number of ambitious but necessary targets. Current efforts are designed to increase the size of the existing wild population and to establish two further self-sustaining reintroduced populations. An important part of the conservation plan is to ensure that the self-sustaining populations in the wild grow to at least 1,000 birds.

**The whooping crane** is a huge white crane that is threatened by the high incidence of collisions with powerlines among fledglings. A recent experiment aimed at making the lines more visible has reduced collisions by 40 to 60 percent.

# Takahe

*Porphyrio hochstetteri*

*Once believed extinct, the flightless takahe of New Zealand was rediscovered in 1948 in the cold, wet, and remote mountains of Fiordland on South Island. Since then its numbers have fluctuated fairly constantly between 100 and 300, but a recent steady increase offers hope for the future.*

Isolated in the South Pacific, between the coral seas of Polynesia and the windswept pack ice of Antarctica, New Zealand has been cut off from the rest of the world for 80 million years. Inaccessible to the mammals that spread over other regions of the world during this time, it became the home of an extraordinary variety of birds adapted for every conceivable lifestyle. Since the birds had no need to escape from enemies such as cats, foxes, or humans, many of them lacked any fear of predators and the power of flight.

One of the most spectacular of these flightless islanders is the takahe, a giant bird that once ranged all over the North and South Islands, originally occurring throughout the islands' forests and grasslands. Its troubles began with the arrival of

Polynesian colonists about 1,000 years ago. These colonists—the Maori—found the takahe easy meat and probably wiped out local populations by hunting them. This probably drove the birds into suboptimal grassland habitats, where there was little hunting.

The Maori also brought the first of many mammal invaders: pigs, rats, and dogs. Some 800 years later European settlers arrived and began introducing a whole menagerie of cats, foxes, stoats, possums, rabbits, deer, cattle, and sheep to the islands. While predators such as the stoat attacked the takahe, the grazers destroyed its food supply. By degrees the takahe disappeared, and by the 1930s the species was believed to be extinct.

## DATA PANEL

**Takahe (notornis)**

*Porphyrio hochstetteri*

**Family:** Rallidae

**World population:** About 230 birds

**Distribution:** Occurs naturally on South Island, New Zealand, but has been introduced to 4 predator-free islands off New Zealand

**Habitat:** Mountain tussock grassland in summer; beech forest and scrub in winter

**Size:** Length: 25 in (63 cm). Weight: male 4.8–8.8 lb (2.2–4 kg); female 4–7.7 lb (1.8–3.5 kg)

**Form:** A bulky, flightless bird with a large red bill and frontal shield, reduced wings, and a short tail. Head and neck iridescent blue; peacock-blue shoulders; green and blue back and wings; red legs. Juveniles duller

**Diet:** Mainly juices from the tender bases of snow tussock grasses; grass seeds and fern rhizomes in winter; also some insects and s mall lizards

**Breeding:** Pairs mate for life and usually breed October–December. A nest is built on the ground; 2 brown-blotched, pale-buff eggs are incubated for 4–4.5 weeks by both parents. Chicks depend on parents for 4 months

**Related endangered species:** One of 33 threatened species in the family Rallidae, including Invisible rail (*Habroptila wallacii*) VU; Guam rail (*Gallirallus owstoni*) EW; Makira moorhen (*Gallinula sylvestris*) CR; Samoan moorhen (*G. pacifica*) CR; and horned coot (*Fulica cornuta*) NT

**Status:** IUCN EN

*Tiritiri Matangi Island*

*North Island*

**NEW ZEALAND**

*Islands of Kapiti, Mana, and Maud*

*South Island*

*Murchison and Stuart Mountains*

## Rediscovery

In fact, the takahe had retreated to the remote Murchison Mountains in the Fiordland of South Island. When it was rediscovered in 1948, there were between 250 and 300 birds left, surviving in a region of heavy snows and high rainfall. It is a hard life, and it has been made harder by introduced red deer that overgraze and eliminate the most nutritious grasses, leaving little for the takahe to eat. The takahe also suffers predation by stoats, and as a result it has a low breeding success rate. Between 1980 and 2000 the wild population fluctuated at levels between 100 and 160 birds, and without intensive conservation actions its chances of survival would have been slim. By 2008 numbers had risen to 300 but then a stoat plague reduced the population again to 230.

## Conservation

Red deer have been controlled in the Murchison Mountains since the 1960s, but despite this the takahe population failed to recover. In an effort to boost its numbers, a captive-breeding unit was established in the 1980s and captive-bred birds were released into the wild. From 1984 to 1991 small populations were also established on four predator-free islands and intensively managed to maximize their breeding success.

There is a plan to establish a second mainland population. The ultimate goal is to reach a total, self-sustaining population of over 500 birds; if the recovery program achieves this, the takahe will be off the Endangered list, but will be classified as Vulnerable.

**The takahe** *is the largest and one of the most colorful members of the rail family.*

# Kakapo

## *Strigops habroptilus*

*Conservationists saved this extraordinary parrot by translocating the few remaining birds to predator-free islands, but the population is still extremely small and inherently at risk.*

The kakapo is the heaviest parrot, one of the few nocturnal species in its family, and the only one that is completely flightless. It lives mainly on the ground, where its massive legs and feet enable it to travel far and quite fast. It uses its wings to balance when running at speed and climbing up leaning trunks and branches, and to break its fall as it parachutes from branches or down steep slopes. It is incapable of gliding, let alone powered flight.

Like so much about this exceptional parrot, its social life (or lack of it) and reproductive behavior are remarkable. In contrast to other parrots, which are among the most gregarious and sociable of birds, the kakapo is solitary except during courtship, and then the interactions between males are highly aggressive; researchers who kept kakapos together found they would attack and even kill one another.

The kakapo is the only parrot species with a "lek" breeding system, in which several rival males assemble at a shared "arena" on summer nights to attract females to mate with them. This arena consists of a complex system of well-defined paths, linking a number of bowl-shaped depressions in the ground. Both paths and bowls are made by the males, and each male has a bowl of his own. He fits inside it and inflates the air sac within his chest until he swells up like a big green balloon, then releases the air to produce the loud, booming calls that act as a magnet for the waiting females. The bowl amplifies the strange sound, which is audible to humans from up to 3 miles (5 km) away.

Each male has to spend many nights booming—up to 1,000 times an hour—to secure a mate. He also carefully cleans his tracks and bowl, and defends them fiercely against rival males. After mating, a female is on her own. Having laid her eggs, she must incubate them for a month and may care for the young for a further nine months. All this activity requires a great deal of energy from both sexes. It is hardly surprising, then, that kakapos do not breed every year, but only irregularly at intervals of three to five years, triggered by the periodic abundance (known as "masting") of seeds and fruit of certain key plant species, such as the native rimu tree.

### To the Brink of Extinction

Evidence from preserved bones shows that for some time after the first Maori settlers arrived in New Zealand about 1,000 years ago, the kakapo was found throughout most of the country. However, with the Maori colonization of the land the kakapo's range started contracting. The birds suffered as the settlers altered habitats, and especially as they introduced dogs and Pacific rats, which hunted down the birds— as did the Maori themselves. The Maori ate them and also valued their feathers for making cloaks.

Evolving on a group of oceanic islands that had no native mammalian predators (New Zealand lacks any native mammals apart from three species of bat), the kakapo had no need to evolve defenses against them and so was especially vulnerable. Kakapo mothers had to search for food at night, leaving their eggs and chicks unattended and so even more vulnerable.

After Europeans colonized New Zealand from the early 19th century, they introduced other carnivorous mammals such as stoats, cats, dogs, black and brown rats, and Australian brush-tailed possums. These animals caused even more devastation among kakapo populations. By 1976 only 18 birds were known to exist in the remote mountain country of Fiordland, in the southwest corner of South Island, and all of them were males. By 1989 the Fiordland birds—the last mainland population—were gone. However, in 1977 the dramatic discovery was made of about 150 kakapos living on Stewart Island, the largest of New Zealand's offshore islands. Over half the birds were being killed each year by feral cats. Between 1980 and 1992 the 61 kakapos on Stewart Island were moved to predator-free offshore islands.

Today kakapos are tagged with miniature radio transmitters, and every nest is constantly monitored using infrared video cameras. Kakapo eggs and nestlings are kept warm with heating pads when the females leave to forage at night. Providing extra food has increased the frequency and the success of breeding attempts, and researchers are currently investigating whether rimu trees can be induced to fruit using plant hormones.

Thanks to the work of conservationists and to a run of three successful breeding seasons, the kakapo population is at last increasing. In the breeding season of 2008–2009 the population exceeded 100, and by February 2010 there were 122 birds. Even so, there is a long way to go before the kakapo is secure.

**The kakapo** *is a giant, flightless parrot that resembles an owl in its facial disks (Strigops means "owl face").*

## DATA PANEL

**Kakapo (owl parrot)**

*Strigops habroptilus*

**Family:** Psittacidae

**World population:** 122 birds

**Distribution:** Translocated birds on 4 New Zealand offshore islands: Maud, Inner Chetwode, Codfish, and Pearl

**Habitat:** Mainly forest edges and forests in younger stages of growth

**Size:** Length: 23–25 in (58–64 cm); wingspan: 33–36 in (84–91 cm)

**Form:** Large, stout-bodied parrot with hairlike facial disk, short, broad bill with cere (bare skin at base containing nostrils) prominent and swollen; short, broad wings; scruffy, downcurved tail; massive, fleshy legs and feet with powerful claws; plumage moss-green on upperparts and greenish-yellow on underparts; mottled and barred with brown and yellowish; male has wider head and much bigger bill and is about 25% heavier than female

**Diet:** Leaves, stems, roots, fruit, nectar, and seeds of trees, shrubs, etc.

**Breeding:** Breeds every 2–5 years, coinciding with bumper crops of food plants; nests inside rotting fallen tree trunks, in hollow tree stumps, or under clumps of vegetation; 1–3 white eggs incubated by the female for 30 days; fledging period 10–12 weeks; may not attain sexual maturity until 6–9 years old

**Related endangered species:** There are no other members of the subgroup Strigopini, but 2 other threatened New Zealand parrots, the kaka (*Nestor meridionalis*) EN and kea (*N. notabilis*) VU, may be related; some experts think that the kakapo may be related to the night parrot (*Pezoporus occidentalis*) CR and the ground parrot (*Pezoporus wallicus*) of Australia LR

**Status:** IUCN CR

North Island

NEW ZEALAND

Islands of Maud and Inner Chetwode

South Island

Codfish Island

Pearl Island

# Hyacinth Macaw

*Anodorhynchus hyacinthinus*

*The world's largest parrot, the hyacinth macaw is a spectacular vivid blue South American bird. It has suffered a massive decline in numbers over the last 40 years due mainly to illegal trapping for private collectors.*

Once relatively numerous across much of its range in Brazil, the hyacinth macaw is now rare in most of its former strongholds. The largest population occurs in the Brazilian part of the Pantanal region—a huge, grassy plain about the size of Iowa that straddles the southwestern Brazilian states of Mato Grosso and Mato Grosso do Sul, extending southeast into Bolivia and Paraguay. Dotted with palms and other trees and shrubs, the habitat is flooded during the rainy season, peaking in about February to become the biggest freshwater wetland in the world. Even here numbers of the great blue parrots have declined alarmingly in recent times.

The two other, smaller, populations are in the Gerais region of central Brazil and in Amazonia.

In contrast to most of the more familiar macaws of the genus *Ara*, such as the blue-and-yellow and scarlet macaws, which eat a wide range of plants, hyacinth macaws depend on a few species of palm trees for their staple diet of palm nuts.

The massive black bill of the hyacinth macaw is an adaptation to its specialized diet. Accounting for about one-fifth of the entire weight of the bird and worked by powerful muscles, it is immensely strong and forms an impressive and efficient tool for crushing the large, hard nuts of palm trees.

As well as taking them straight from the trees, the birds also feed on the palm nuts where they have fallen on the ground. On ranchlands where cattle are raised they can take advantage of concentrations of palm nuts that remain undigested in cowpats. The cattle digest the soft, fleshy mesocarp surrounding each nut, thereby saving the birds the effort.

Although birds in northeastern Brazil nest on remote cliff crevices, most hyacinth macaws need suitable nesting trees if they are to breed. In the Pantanal only a few of the trees grow big enough to have developed large hollows in which the birds can conceal their nests from predators. However, such big trees and big birds are so prominent that local people cannot fail to be aware of the nest sites. Sometimes, trappers return year after year to steal chicks, while other long-established nesting trees are felled or burned by landowners clearing the land for cattle; both scenarios spell disaster for the hyacinth macaws.

Habitat in the Gerais region is being rapidly converted to mechanized agriculture, cattle ranches, and exotic tree plantations.

## Illegal Trade

During the period between 1970 and 1980 huge numbers of young hyacinth macaws were taken from their nests and sold to dealers or middlemen, who then sold them on to private collectors in the United States, Europe, Japan, and other countries. Some illegal trade still exists. An equal but persistent demand for captive macaws within Brazil, and the taking of birds for feather headdresses or food adds to the problem, despite Brazilian legislation protecting the species. Estimates suggest that up to 10,000 hyacinth macaws may have been taken from the wild in the 1980s alone.

In 1987 the situation regarding international trade was judged to be so serious that the hyacinth macaw was moved from Appendix II to Appendix I of CITES, but for a while this had the unfortunate effect of

## DATA PANEL

**Hyacinth macaw** (hyacinthine macaw, blue macaw, black macaw)

*Anodorhynchus hyacinthinus*

**Family:** Psittacidae

**World population:** About 6,500 individuals, mostly in Brazil; perhaps fewer than 100 in Bolivia; small numbers in Paraguay

**Distribution:** Three main areas of interior Brazil: on the southern side of the Amazon in the northeast; the Gerais region of central Brazil; the seasonally flooded Pantanal region of the Upper Río Paraguay basin, just extending into eastern Bolivia and northern Paraguay

**Habitat:** Lightly wooded areas, especially where clumps of trees are mixed with open grassland or swamps

**Size:** Length: 35–39 in (90–100 cm)

**Form:** Bird of great size with huge, hooked black bill; long, narrow wings; long tail; cobalt-blue plumage, purple on wings and tail, blackish on underwings and undertail

**Diet:** Mainly nuts of various palm trees; fruit, including figs; occasionally water snails; liquid from unripe palm fruits

**Breeding:** Usually in dry season; 2 (rarely 1 or 3) eggs laid; incubation 3–4 weeks, fledging about 3.5 months

**Related endangered species:** Lear's macaw (*Anodorhynchus leari*) EN; glaucous macaw (*A. glaucus*) CR; Spix's macaw (*Cyanopsitta spixii*) CR; blue-throated macaw (*Ara glaucogularis*) CR; military macaw (*A. militaris*) VU; red-fronted macaw (*A. rubrogenys*) EN

**Status:** IUCN EN

stimulating even greater demand by unscrupulous dealers and collectors willing to pay up to $12,000 for each bird.

Recent efforts to save the hyacinth macaw have included studies of its ecology, an investigation into trade in the bird, and the establishment of nest boxes. Most encouragingly, many ranch owners in the Pantanal and Gerais regions no longer allow trapping on their properties.

**The hyacinth macaw** *is a slow breeder, taking about five months from egg-laying to fledging (the time when the young start to fly). The birds rarely succeed in rearing more than one of the usual two chicks.*

# Pink Pigeon

## *Columba (Streptopelia) mayeri*

*Thanks to the dedicated work of conservationists, the pink pigeon has been saved from extinction, and numbers have dramatically increased over the last decade. But without continued intensive management, including a captive-breeding program, the species would be likely to become extinct.*

A close relative of the abundant and widespread wood pigeon of Europe and parts of Asia, the pink pigeon is one of the most attractive members of the large family of pigeons and doves. This group has suffered more than most from extinction, with almost a third of the 309 surviving species classified as Threatened or Lower Risk, near threatened. Over 80 percent of them are island species, as were all but one of the 13 species of pigeons and doves that have recently become extinct.

The pink pigeon is found only on the island of Mauritius and the neighboring Ile aux Aigrettes. Discoveries of bones of the birds indicate that it was once widespread in forests throughout the whole of Mauritius. Now it is confined to the southwestern part of the island. The precarious position the species is in today is entirely due to a variety of human factors.

## Multiple Threats

Along with many other unique animals and plants, the pink pigeon has suffered from the massive destruction of the native forests of Mauritius by colonists from the late 18th century onward. Uncontrolled hunting also played its part in reducing the species to a perilously low and fragmented population.

In addition, the pink pigeon—and other unique Mauritian wildlife—has been affected by predation by the legion of animals deliberately introduced or accidentally brought to the island by sailors and settlers. They include the crab-eating macaque, originally from Southeast Asia, which preys on adult pigeons, also taking eggs and young from their nests. The small Indian mongoose, which was introduced to

control black rats, also preys on young pigeons. However, black rats that take the pigeon's eggs and young have survived and prospered; feral cats are also predators of pigeons.

Other threats affecting the birds include disease and shortages of suitable food in late winter. The remaining small and fragmented populations and their forest habitat are increasingly at the mercy of tropical cyclones that hit the island from time to time. Winds blowing at up to 155 miles per hour (250 km/h) or more not only damage the forest by stripping trees of the shoots and fruit on which the pigeons feed but also blow down the bird's nests.

By 1990, as a result of all these factors, the total world population of this once common species was reduced to just 10 individuals, all of which nested in a single grove of introduced Japanese red cedar trees.

## Rescue Plans

The pink pigeon has been the focus of a major international rescue program for many years. It has involved sponsorship by BirdLife International (a global partnership of conservation organizations), the World Wide Fund for Nature, and the New York Zoological Society. There is also a long-term program of research and rescue involving the Mauritian government working together with several zoos—the Durrell Wildlife Conservation Trust, Vogelpark Walsrode in Germany, and the New York and Alberquerque zoos.

Attempts at captive breeding at the zoos began in the mid-1970s. Careful reintroduction into the wild has recently helped achieve a dramatic increase in the pigeon's numbers. Other elements in the program

## DATA PANEL

**Pink pigeon** (Mauritius pink pigeon, chestnut-tailed pigeon)

*Columba (Streptopelia) mayeri*

**Family:** Columbidae

**World population:** 395 birds

**Distribution:** Restricted to 4 sites in southwestern Mauritius and introduced to Ile aux Aigrettes, off eastern coast

**Habitat:** Subtropical evergreen forests, including remnant native trees and introduced species; most pairs nest in introduced Japanese red cedars

**Size:** Length:14–14.8 in (36–40 cm). Weight: male 8.5–14.5 oz (240–410 g); female 7.5–13 oz (213–369 g)

**Form:** Slightly larger than feral pigeon, with smaller head, larger body, and broad, rounded wings; plumage pink-white; duskier on upper back, belly, flanks, and undertail; rest of upperparts and wings dark chocolate-brown; primary flight feathers darker; lower back and rump blue-gray; uppertail coverts and tail red-orange or chestnut; eyes surrounded by red ring of bare skin with white or pale-yellow iris; bill red at base with a creamy tip; red feet

**Diet:** Wide variety of fruit and berries as well as leaves and flowers

**Breeding:** Nest is platform of twigs; 2 white eggs incubated for 13–18 days; young fledge in about 20 days

**Related endangered species:** Sixty-one species of pigeons are threatened, 17 of these in the genus *Columba*, including silvery wood pigeon (*C. argentina*) CR; yellow-legged pigeon (*C. pallidiceps*) VU; and white-tailed laurel pigeon (*C. junoniae*) EN

**Status:** IUCN EN

include restoring habitat, controlling introduced predators and guarding nests to prevent predation, rescuing eggs and young from failing nests, providing the birds with extra food, and controlling disease.

The rescue program came barely in time to save the pink pigeon. The intensive management has seen a dramatic increase in the numbers of the pigeons. A few more years of decline and the species would probably have suffered the same fate as its closest relative, the long-extinct Réunion pigeon.

**The pink pigeon**

*has undergone a remarkable improvement in status. Once classified by the IUCN as Critically Endangered, it was downgraded to Endangered in 2000, a status that was confirmed in 2004.*

# Spotted Owl

## *Strix occidentalis*

*Largely restricted to the ancient conifer and oak forests that once extended all along the Pacific coast of North America, the spotted owl is being driven from its ancestral habitats by logging operations that target the biggest, oldest, and most valuable trees.*

Found in four distinct populations from southwestern Canada to Mexico, the spotted owl is primarily a bird of mature, moist, temperate forests. Throughout its range it is a night hunter that uses its acute hearing and night-adapted eyesight to pinpoint small mammals and birds in the darkness as it perches above the forest floor. Swooping down on silent wings, it seizes its victim in its feathered talons and returns to the perch to sever its spinal cord with its bill. Then it swallows the prey whole, headfirst.

The forests of great redwoods, pines, hemlocks, cedars, and oaks provide the spotted owl with a wealth of prey and plenty of quiet roosting sites where it can spend the day undisturbed.

They also offer ideal nesting holes in big, mature trees, although the owl will sometimes use a rock cavity or even an abandoned squirrel nest. Many spotted owls stay on their nesting territories throughout the year, defending them against trespassing rivals with loud whoops and shrieks that echo through the forest. It is an eerie, evocative, and increasingly rare sound.

### Logged Out

As is the case elsewhere, ancient forests of western North America are being destroyed for their timber. Secondary forest is no replacement for the rich, multilayered patchwork of trees, shrubs, and undergrowth that develops naturally over the centuries. It does not have the same diversity of wildlife—which for the spotted owl means prey—and the young trees lack holes and snags where birds can

## DATA PANEL

**Spotted owl**

*Strix occidentalis*

**Family:** Strigidae

**World population:** About 15,000 birds in 4 races

**Distribution:** Western North America: northern race *S. o. caurina* from southern British Columbia to northern California; California race *S. o. occidentalis* through central and southern California; Mexican race *S. o. lucida* scattered from southern Utah to central Mexico; the fourth, from the State of Mexico in southern central Mexico, recently described and named *juanaphillipsae*

**Habitat:** Mainly moist, temperate old-growth conifer or oak forest, but Mexican race also occurs in warmer, drier, secondary pine-oak forest and rocky canyons

**Size:** Length: 16–19 in (41–48 cm). Weight: 1.1–1.7 lb (520–760 g)

**Form:** Medium-sized, upright, round-headed owl with well-defined facial disk, black eyes, and fully feathered feet. Upperparts rich red-brown, with white spots on head and neck; mottled buff on back and wings; underparts barred whitish and rust-brown. Mexican race paler. Juvenile pale brown with dark barring

**Diet:** Mainly small mammals; also roosting birds (including small owls) and insects

**Breeding:** Birds pair for life, nesting March–June. Usually 2 eggs, laid on bare floor of tree cavity or crevice and incubated by female for 30 days. Downy chicks brooded by female for 2 weeks while male brings food, then both parents forage; fledged young leave nest at 35 days

**Related endangered species:** Twenty-three other owls in the family Strigidae, including Blakiston's fish owl *(Ketupa blakistoni)* EN; São Tomé scops-owl *(Otus hartlaubi)* VU; Sokoke scops-owl *(O. ireneae)* EN; rufous fishing-owl *(Scotopelia ussheri)* EN; and long-whiskered owlet *(Xenoglaux loweryi)* EN

**Status:** IUCN NT

nest and perch. Spotted owls avoid plantations that are fewer than 100 years old, and a forest has to be at least 200 years old for it to become suitable breeding habitat.

The old trees are the biggest and most valuable. Consequently, tracts of prime old-growth forest have been clear-felled, leaving nothing but stumps. Where big trees are more scattered, they are often selectively felled to leave younger, smaller trees. Both strategies are catastrophic for the owl, especially the northern race. It is estimated that in the northwestern United States the degree of spotted owl habitat loss ranges from 54 percent to over 99 percent.

Logging and the spread of farmland and towns, reservoir development, and mining have led to a steep decline in the population of spotted owls. There are some 8,500 of the northern race surviving in the huge swath of coastal forest from Canada to northern California. The California race is in trouble too, with about 3,000 left. The more adaptable Mexican race numbers up to 1,500 in the American part of its range, with perhaps 2,000 in Mexico itself; the southern owls seem to be holding their own, partly because they are less tied to old-growth forest, but also because they are not suffering such heavy habitat losses.

The spotted owl is classified as Lower Risk, near threatened rather than Endangered, but its decline is accelerating, and it has become the subject of six management plans in Canada and the United States. It has also been the focus of a heated debate between conservationists, timber companies, and politicians over the future of the forests.

**The spotted owl** *like many other nocturnal owl species, has a facial disk that helps reflect sound to the ears, helping the birds locate prey.*

# Bee Hummingbird

## Mellisuga helenae

*Bee hummingbirds are found only on the island of Cuba, and the males of the species are famous for being the world's smallest living bird. Although they were once relatively common and widespread, they are now becoming increasingly rare and localized.*

As its name suggests, the bee hummingbird can easily be mistaken for a large bee as it hovers to sip nectar from the blossom of a hibiscus plant or an aloe. About half of its diminutive length is taken up by its long, slender bill and short tail. Among the smallest of all vertebrate animals, it weighs about 75,000 times less than the world's largest bird, the male ostrich, and is about the same size as an ostrich eye. Bee hummingbirds are dwarfed by many of the butterflies found in their tropical forest home.

Like other hummingbirds, the bee hummingbird feeds in flight. It is a superb flyer and has wings with bones that are fused except at the shoulder joint. This wing design enables it to rotate its wings. Such prowess in the air allows it to hover in one spot, remaining almost motionless in front of a flower to feed. It can also fly sideways, straight up and down, and even backward.

When hovering, a bee hummingbird beats its wings 70 times per second. This uses up large amounts of energy—and such a tiny animal can store very little. Consequently, it must have a constant source of energy-rich food that it can convert quickly into fuel to power its proportionately large wing muscles and maintain its high metabolism. It finds this food in the form of nectar, which it sips from tubular flowers by inserting its long, slender bill and lapping up the sugary liquid with its long, grooved tongue. The bee hummingbird needs to feed every few minutes. It can only survive short periods without food, and it does so by becoming torpid, reducing its metabolic rate by 80 to 90 percent and thereby saving up to 60 percent of its energy requirements. The male bee hummingbird is fiercely territorial, driving off any intruder of the same or different species that attempts to feed from his patch of nectar-rich flowers.

### Spectacular Displays

A male attracts a mate in three ways. First, he expands his gorget—a bib of feathers—and lateral plumes, which take on a glittering, jewellike appearance in sunlight and are iridescent—the colors change depending on the viewing angle.

## DATA PANEL

**Bee hummingbird**

*Mellisuga helenae*

**Family:** Trochilidae

**World population:** Over 10,000 birds (estimated), declining

**Distribution:** Cuba; formerly occurred on the Isla de la Juventud (Isle of Youth) to the southwest of Cuba

**Habitat:** Mainly coastal forests and forest margins, with thick tangles of lianas and abundant epiphytes (plants that grow on other plants); also interior forests, wooded mountain valleys, swamps, and gardens

**Size:** Length: 2–2.3 in (5–6 cm); male slightly smaller than female. Weight: 0.05–0.07 oz (1.6–1.9 g)

**Form:** Tiny bird with long, straight, black bill. Male's head, throat, lateral plumes, and gorget (bib of feathers) glitter fiery red in sunlight; rest of upperparts bluish; rest of underparts off-white. Female and immatures have green upperparts and whitish underparts

**Diet:** Adults eat nectar from a wide range of flowers; also small insects

**Breeding:** Season from March to June. Female weaves nest from dried plant fibers, camouflaged on the outside with lichens, usually partly hidden by leaves and lined with soft plant wool; 2 white eggs incubated for 21–22 days. Young fledge at 13–14 days, leaving nest at about 18 days

**Related endangered species:** No close relatives, but 9 hummingbird species classed as Critical, 9 as Endangered, and 9 as Vulnerable

**Status:** IUCN NT

UNITED STATES
BAHAMAS
Isla de Juventud
CUBA
Cayman Islands (U.K.)
JAMAICA

Second, he zooms around in an aerial display. Third, he beats his wings to make a humming noise.

Pairs of birds mate in flight, after which the female builds a tiny, deep, cup-shaped nest in a forked twig or on a branch of a tree. Into it she lays two pea-sized eggs. She must keep the young supplied with a nourishing diet of nectar and partly digested insects.

## Threatened Habitat

The bee hummingbird was once found throughout Cuba and the Isla de la Juventud (Isle of Youth) to the southwest of Cuba. Today it may survive only in a few sites in La Habana, Sierra de Anafe, Guanahacabibes Peninsula, Zapata Swamp, Moa, Mayarí, and the coast of Guantánamo. The bird seems to be heavily dependent on mature forest.

Much of Cuba's native vegetation has been converted for growing crops or for cattle pasture, and only 15 to 20 percent of the land remains in its natural state. Large areas of rain forest have been destroyed to make way for plantations of cacao, coffee, and tobacco, while dry forest is threatened by logging, charcoal production, and slash-and-burn cultivation. In the Zapata Swamp, burning, drainage, and agricultural expansion take their toll.

Although there are some 200 conservation areas in Cuba, making up about 12 percent of the total land area, some are probably too small to support their wildlife, and few afford sufficient protection from logging and other threats. Conservation efforts must be improved to save the bee hummingbird.

**The bee hummingbird** *beats its wings 70 times per second when feeding.*

# Regent Honeyeater

## *Xanthomyza phrygia*

*The strikingly patterned regent honeyeater has suffered serious declines in range and numbers as a result of the destruction and fragmentation of its forest habitat, and probably also because it has lost out in competition with more adaptable rivals.*

The honeyeater family is one of the major groups of Australian birds. Almost 40 percent of the 170 species in the world occur in Australia; the family evolved there and in New Guinea. At least one species occurs in every different land habitat in Australia, and 10 or more species may occur in a single area: Honeyeaters may account for over half of all the birds in a locality.

### Brush Tongues

The most distinctive adaptation of the regent honeyeater is its brush-tipped tongue. When the bird pushes its beak into a flower and extends its tongue beyond the beak's tip, the tongue laps up nectar or other sugary fluids the way a paint-brush collects paint. Most honeyeaters can lap up all the nectar from a flower in less than a second. This adaptation is a major factor in the group's success.

Nevertheless, some species of honeyeater are not thriving. One of the most threatened is the regent honeyeater. This attractive and characterful bird feeds on nectar mainly from the flowers of trees—red ironbark, yellow gum and other eucalypts, and yellow box. The bird also eats manna (a sugary sap produced on tree bark in response to injury, especially by insects) and lerps (or honeydew), as well as fruit. All the foods are rich in energy but low in nutrients, so the birds have to spend a lot of time feeding; they live a partly nomadic life, moving around to find the best feeding

## DATA PANEL

**Regent honeyeater**

*Xanthomyza phrygia*

**Family:** Meliphagidae

**World population:** About 1,500 birds

**Distribution:** Southeastern Australia; mainly at a few sites in northeastern Victoria, along the western slopes of the Great Dividing Range and central coast of New South Wales, with only small numbers elsewhere; now extinct in South Australia

**Habitat:** Dry, open forests and woodlands, especially those dominated by yellow box, red ironbark, and yellow gum trees; also riverside forests of river she-oaks in New South Wales

**Size:** Length: 8–9.5 in (20–24 cm)

**Form:** Slim-bodied, thrush-sized bird with downcurved, sharp-tipped bill; long tail. Male has black head, neck, upper back, and upper breast; patch of bare, pink or yellow skin around each eye; rest of upperparts black with pale-yellow scaly pattern; wings black with broad white fringes to some coverts; 3 broad yellow panels in each folded wing; lower breast, upper belly, and flanks creamy with black chevrons, rest of underparts white; tail black above with yellow edges and tip, bright yellow below. Female smaller and duller. Juvenile browner with yellow bill

**Diet:** Nectar from various flowers; also insects, manna (sugary sap produced by trees in response to injury), lerps (or honeydew—sugary secretions of aphids and plant-eating insects), and fruit, including mistletoe berries

**Breeding:** Mainly August–January (may not nest some years); nest of bark and grass strips lined with plant down and hair, built in tree 6.5–33 ft (2–10 m) tall, in an upright fork or among mistletoe; 2–3 salmon-buff eggs with red-brown spots; incubation about 15 days; fledging period about 14 days

**Related endangered species:** Crow honeyeater (*Gymnomyza aubryana*) CR; black-eared miner (*Manorina melanotis*) EN; stitchbird (*Notiomystis cincta*) VU; dusky friarbird (*Philemon fuscicapillus*) VU; long-bearded melidectes (*Melidectes princeps*) VU; painted honeyeater (*Grantiella picta*) VU; white-chinned myzomela (*Myzomela albigula*) DD; Chatham Island bellbird (*Anthornis melanocephala*) EX

**Status:** IUCN EN

sites. When breeding, they need more protein, and they include insects in their diet in order to satisfy this requirement. They take them from the trunks, branches, or foliage of trees, but sometimes catch them in flight.

Honeyeaters are quarrelsome birds, often chasing away rivals of their own and other species from flowering trees and other plants. It has been discovered that regent honeyeaters mimic the calls of larger species of honeyeater, such as friarbirds, wattlebirds, and the spiny-cheeked honeyeater, in an attempt to prevent these more dominant relatives from driving them away from sources of nectar.

## Fragmented Forests

Despite the skilled mimicry, fragmentation of the regent honeyeater's habitat seems to be favoring more aggressive species, such as the noisy miner, which may be replacing the regent honeyeater in parts of its range. The habitat loss may be affecting the less adaptable regent honeyeater to such an extent that it is unable to gather in sufficient numbers at breeding sites to share the effort of driving rivals away from good nectar sources. Today only about a quarter of its habitat remains, the rest having been cleared for agriculture, timber, and other developments. What remains is often of inferior quality, with larger trees removed and an increasing number of unhealthy trees.

In many places the regent honeyeater appears only sporadically. When breeding, the birds are concentrated at relatively few sites, but numbers fluctuate greatly between sites and from one year to the next. In places where they have been scarce or absent for years they may suddenly return in large numbers. Years when few or no birds breed at a site may be a result of their failure to nest or because they have moved elsewhere to breed. Little is known about the birds' movements outside the breeding season.

**The regent honeyeater**, *an attractive, brightly plumaged bird, lives, feeds and breeds in dry, open forests.*

Conservationists carry out annual surveys of the species' range and abundance. A captive colony has now been established. Logging and grazing have been restricted at some major sites, and many of the trees favored by the honeyeaters have been planted to replace those destroyed or in poor health.

Plans to build on this work include studying the movements and population dynamics of the species, measuring the degree of isolation between different breeding populations, assessing the effect of noisy miners, and surveying and monitoring the birds' habitat to ensure that it is not degraded.

# Blue Bird of Paradise

### *Paradisaea rudolphi*

*One of the most beautiful species in a family containing many spectacular-looking birds, the blue bird of paradise is also one of the most threatened—mainly by the loss of its habitat, but also by hunting for the stunning blue display plumes of the male.*

As with many other birds of paradise, male blue birds of paradise are among the most stunning-looking birds in the world. An adult male is adorned with brilliant blue and violet filmy plumes that cascade from tufts of deep-crimson flank plumes on either side of his belly. In addition, two exceptionally long central tail feathers extend like narrow black ribbons and end in bright-blue spatula shapes. Over millions of years competition between rival males to appeal to females has led to the evolution of increasingly spectacular plumage and dramatic courtship displays.

Having prepared a special display site by stripping leaves from the surrounding branches, the male hangs upside down by his feet from a branch and gently sways back and forth. At the same time, he expands his iridescent display plumes to shimmer in the sunlight that penetrates the forest canopy. His scarlet-bordered black belly patch pulsates as he moves. After a few minutes he narrows his eyes to emphasize the white patches above and below them. All the while he utters an extraordinary buzzing, crackling, and whirring song, which sounds like radio static.

The gorgeous plumes and amazing display are the badge of adult males. The plumage of immature males resembles that of females, but with longer, narrower central tail feathers that grow with age. As the males mature, they also acquire more blue and violet feathers that will equip them to perform the displays.

## Patchy Distribution

The blue bird of paradise is found only on the island of New Guinea. It is restricted to forests in the eastern Central Ranges in Papua New Guinea on the eastern half of the island. It is not known why the species' range does not extend into Papua, the Indonesian province on the western half of the island.

Within its limited range the blue bird of paradise is common in some areas, but rare or patchy in many places and absent from others—especially on the northern slopes of the southeastern mountains. The male blue bird of paradise spends much of his life defending his territories and attracting mates. Males

## DATA PANEL

**Blue bird of paradise**

*Paradisaea rudolphi*

**Family:** Paradiseidae

**World population:** Estimated at 2,500–10,000 birds

**Distribution:** Papua New Guinea, in mountains of eastern Central Ranges

**Habitat:** Mainly montane primary oak forest, forest edge, and older secondary growth at lower levels 4,600–5,900 ft (1,400–1,800 m)

**Size:** Length: male 26 in (67 cm), including elongated tail feathers; female 12 in (30 cm). Weight: 4–7 oz (124–189 g)

**Form:** Pigeon-sized bird with dark plumage, white eye-ring, and stout, blue-white bill; male has glossy black plumage with blue feathers on wings, lower back, and tail; long, gauzelike plumes; 2 central feathers in tail form long ribbons with spatula-shaped tips. Female lacks ornamental plumes and has chestnut underparts

**Diet:** Mainly fruit, including figs, wild peppers, and wild bananas; also insects, including crickets, and spiders

**Breeding:** Nest bowl built in tree or bush; usually 1 pale-pink egg with lavender-gray and brown markings; incubated by female for about 18 days; young cared for by female alone

**Related endangered species:** Three other birds of paradise: MacGregor's bird of paradise (*Macgregoria pulchra*) VU; black sicklebill (*Epimachus fastuosus*) VU; Wahne's parotia (*Parotia wahnesi*) VU

**Status:** IUCN VU

INDONESIA • New Guinea • PAPUA NEW GUINEA • AUSTRALIA

are usually found only in primary forest, but some have been seen in fragmented areas of primary forest or in secondary forest. Female-plumaged birds (immature males or females) are often seen at the edge of the forest, and in areas of denser, older secondary growth.

Typically, there is also an altitude difference in the distribution of male and female blue birds of paradise; mature males occupy the central portion of the habitat, between 4,600 and 5,900 feet (1,400 and 1,800 m), and the female-plumaged birds tend to live in the upper and lower edges of the forest, up to 6,600 feet (2,000 m) and down to 3,600 feet (1,100 m).

Adult males are essentially solitary birds, but female-plumaged birds are sometimes encountered in small groups feeding at fruit-bearing trees. They may also feed with other species of bird of paradise. Although they find some fruit high in the forest canopy, most feeding occurs at lower levels, and individuals have been recorded foraging to within 3.3 to 6.6 feet (1 to 2 m) of the ground. While the bulk of their diet is the fruit of many different trees and shrubs, they also eat insects, including cockroaches, grasshoppers, and spiders.

## Forest Clearance and Hunting

In the 1950s researchers looked at the distribution of the blue bird of paradise and recorded that it had gone from huge areas of forest that had been cleared for subsistence agriculture. Habitat loss still poses a major threat to the species today. Unfortunately, its range lies entirely within the zone most favored in Papua New Guinea for new settlements, agriculture, and logging.

Hunting is another threat. The species has been hunted by the islanders for hundreds of years for its spectacular plumes, which are used in headdresses and other ritual ornamentation. Where males are regularly hunted, they may abandon an area. The losses from hunting may be compounded by unfavorable competition with the Raggiana bird of paradise, which is better able to adapt to disturbed habitat.

Information about numbers and the rates of decline of the blue bird of paradise is lacking, but records suggest that its total population is relatively small and fragmented into small subpopulations. More data may result in reclassification of the species up to Endangered or down to Lower Risk, near threatened.

## Conservation Priorities

Conservationists have identified several targets for protecting the blue bird of paradise, including pinpointing the species' exact distribution and determining its western, northern, and eastern boundaries. Studies into the effects of habitat change and hunting are ongoing. Other priorities include the enforcement of existing protective legislation and the implementation of various public education programs.

**The male blue bird of paradise** is hunted for its feathers, which are used in headdresses. The bird's appeal should help publicize conservation initiatives.

# Raso Lark

## Alauda razae

*With one of the smallest ranges of any bird in the world, the Raso lark—a close relative of the skylark—is critically threatened by adverse changes on the tiny Atlantic island to which it is restricted. Its total population is currently in the low hundreds or fewer.*

The Raso lark is found only on the islet of Raso (or Razo) in the Cape Verde group, 310 miles (500 km) off the west coast of Africa. Volcanic in origin, Raso is low-lying and lacks natural water supplies. It experiences only slight and erratic rainfall that does nothing to relieve the dry conditions. Although the larger islands in the group have human populations, Raso is uninhabited.

Raso is also small—less than 3 square miles (7 sq. km) in area—and suitable breeding habitat for the lark occupies less than half of the islet's total area. Most of the birds feed and breed on a flat expanse of decomposing volcanic lava and soft rocks deposited from hot, lime-rich springs that support a sparse growth of herbaceous plants and low scrub. Although individuals have sometimes been recorded elsewhere

on the island, the Raso lark has never been recorded anywhere beyond its shores.

Raso larks feed on insects and seeds. Analysis of the stomach contents of two birds collected in the late 1960s showed them to contain ants, beetles, seeds, and other vegetable matter, as well as grit, probably swallowed to aid digestion. Since then the larks have been observed using their bills—which are heavier and longer than those of skylarks—to pry pebbles out of the soil, presumably to expose items of food.

An interesting feature of the species is the difference—of almost 21 percent—in the length of the bill in males and females. The gap has probably evolved in response to the island's relatively meager food resources—plants and animals that depend for their existence primarily

## DATA PANEL

**Raso lark (Razo lark)**

*Alauda razae*

**Family:** Alaudidae

**World population:** 190 mature individuals

**Distribution:** Found only on the tiny island of Raso, in the Cape Verde Island group in the Atlantic off the west coast of Africa

**Habitat:** Mostly volcanic plains with patches of sparse vegetation, where it feeds and breeds; sometimes ventures farther afield to feed

**Size:** Length: 5 in (13 cm); wingspan: 8.5–10 in (22–26 cm)

**Form:** Similar to Eurasian skylark, but less than 75% of its size, with wings that are 30–40% shorter and more rounded; bigger bill, shorter tail,

and proportionately longer legs; short, erectile crest. Plumage dull grayish, with buff and blackish streaks above; blackish tail has white outer feathers; legs brownish pink

**Diet:** Seeds and insects

**Breeding:** Governed by scarce, irregular rainfall; builds fragile nest of grass in small hollows under creeping vegetation or a boulder; eggs whitish, with fine grayish to brownish spots; clutch of 3 recorded. Incubation and fledging periods unknown

**Related endangered species:** Seven other species of larks are threatened, including Rudd's lark (*Heteromirafra ruddi*) VU, Ash's lark (*Mirafra ashi*) EN, and Botha's lark (*Spizocorys fringillaris*) EN

**Status:** IUCN CR

Santo Antão
São Vicente
Raso
Sal
São Nicolau
Boa Vista
**CAPE VERDE**
Maio
Brava
Fogo
São Tiago

on the nutrients provided by the guano (droppings) from seabird colonies. The bill difference enables both sexes to feed on different food items, reducing competition for the limited food supply.

Past records refer to the species as being easy to approach and showing no fear of humans, although more recent observations have suggested that the birds are now somewhat warier.

## Fluctuating Population

Censuses carried out by visiting ornithologists reveal that the Raso lark population has fluctuated over the years. Between the mid-1960s and the early 1980s estimates suggested that there were only between 20 and 50 pairs. However, a survey in early 1985 showed that there were at least 150 birds on the islet, and by 1992 the figure had risen to about 250. When a count was made in 1998, though, the researchers found a total of only 92 birds, restricted to the south and west of the islet, suggesting that the population had contracted in range. In 2009 there were just 190 mature individuals.

Recent droughts are almost certainly responsible for the decline. However, they indicate something other than natural climatic variability. There is evidence of long-term reversion of the land to desert in the Cape Verde Islands, probably as a result of emissions of greenhouse gases. In addition, since the lark nests on the ground, its already small population is in danger of being wiped out by rats, cats, and dogs accidentally carried to the islet by fishermen. A dog was seen on Raso in 1994, and evidence that cats were present was found during the 1998 survey. Signs of nest predation have also been found—the culprit was possibly a brown-necked raven.

Although Raso was declared a nature reserve and given legal protection in 1990, there has been no actual enforcement of protection. To ensure the survival of the Raso lark, it will be essential to check if cats or other predators have become established on the island and, if so, to eradicate them as quickly as possible. Another urgent task for conservationists is to continue to carry out regular surveys, so that they can be alerted to the first signs of further declines.

**The Raso lark** *is found on a single uninhabited island where, until recently, it has been protected by its isolation.*

# Gouldian Finch

## *Erythrura gouldiae*

*Once abundant and widespread over much of northern Australia, the beautiful and colorful Gouldian finch is greatly reduced in numbers and breeding sites, due mainly to habitat changes.*

Records suggest that in the early 20th century the Gouldian finch was a common and familiar member of its family with an extensive range. During the 20th century, however, the species suffered a dramatic decline both in numbers and distribution. During the 1960s a survey at Pine Creek, Cape York, Australia, caught about 1,000 individuals in one week. A second survey in the same area in 1996 found only half a dozen birds in three months.

It is not surprising that such a stunning-looking bird was popular with cage-bird enthusiasts. Large numbers were caught—legally and illegally—for the Australian and international trade in captive birds until the early 1980s. The numbers of birds legally caught each year by licensed bird trappers were recorded until the end of 1986, when the trapping of Gouldian finches was banned. The statistics showed that between 1972 and 1981 there was an 87 percent decline in numbers caught in Western Australia. At the end of this period—five years before the trapping ban—no Gouldian finches were caught commercially. Large-scale trapping is likely to have depleted populations, but landscape changes are thought to be much more significant.

Gouldian finches are primarily birds of open tropical woodland with a grassy understory, where they are highly selective both in their diet and choice of breeding sites. They feed exclusively on grass seeds; the grass species varies seasonally and geographically. The birds travel over large distances to find supplies to build up their reserves before breeding.

### Environmental Change

Gouldian finches are the only members of their family to nest almost exclusively in tree hollows rather than building their own nests. Highly sociable, they breed in loose colonies, preferring clumps of smooth-barked eucalyptus trees, although the species of eucalyptus varies from area to area. At present none of the known breeding sites has long-term protection as a nature reserve.

The Gouldian finch's dependence on a specialized diet makes it sensitive to changes in land management, especially the burning of grasses by farmers. Low-intensity fires

## DATA PANEL

**Gouldian finch (painted finch, rainbow finch, purple-breasted finch, Lady Gould's finch)**

*Erythrura gouldiae*

**Family:** Estrildidae

**World population:** Believed to be between 2,000 and 10,000 mature individuals

**Distribution:** Northern Australia

**Habitat:** Dry savanna grassland; fringes of mangroves and thickets; rarely far from water. Woods and scrubland with spinifex grasses in wet season; avoids human habitation

**Size:** Length: 5–5.5 in (12.5–14 cm). Weight: 0.4–0.5 oz (12–15 g)

**Form:** Multicolored plumage in adults. Male has green upperparts with circular or oval patch on purple breast; yellow belly and flanks; black tail with long, pointed central feathers. Female duller, with shorter central tail feathers. Juveniles have gray heads and lack bright colors and long tail feathers

**Diet:** Ripe and part-ripe grass seeds, mainly sorghum in dry season; seeds of other grasses in the wet season

**Breeding:** Female usually lays 4–8 white eggs directly into tree hollow or termite mound in January–April (rainy season). Incubation 12–13 days; fledging about 21 days

**Related endangered species:** Green-faced parrotfinch (*Erythrura viridifacies*) VU; Shelley's crimson-wing (*Cryptospiza shelleyi*) VU; Anambra waxbill (*Estrilda poliopareia*) VU; green avadavat (*Amandava formosa*) VU

**Status:** IUCN EN

AUSTRALIA

**Gouldian finches** *come in many color varieties. About 75 percent of birds have black faces and 25 percent have crimson heads; there is also a rare yellow-headed form.*

during the dry season can help the birds find food: Fallen seed is more accessible to the birds after any covering of dead stems and leaves has been burned off. At the end of the dry season, however, intense fires burn off tree leaves, destroying suitable shelter. Fierce fires during the wet season can destroy sorghum grassland, including any emerging seedlings. Food shortages after such fires are often made worse by the fact that cattle graze the affected areas, preventing grasses from seeding. Grazing and the uniform fire regime destroy the mosaic of habitats on which the finches depend. The regular burning destroys clumps of breeding trees, and the birds are known to avoid badly burned tree hollows.

## Mite Attack

A symptom of these landscape changes is the high level of infection with a parasitic mite that affects the finch's respiratory system. When birds in captivity are infected, they wheeze and become listless, fail to breed, and die if they are not treated with antibiotics. Although the effects of the mite had not been reported in wild birds, researchers checking for its presence found it occurred in 62 percent of the birds examined. Even though the parasites were not the cause of the massive declines, they may be preventing the species from recovering its numbers.

## Recovery Plan

A recovery plan for the Gouldian finch was announced in 1998. Its chief emphasis was an in-depth study of the ecology and habitat needs of the species. The main objective is to stabilize numbers. Initially the numbers and occurrence of the Gouldian finch must be determined. With a small, scarce bird with a huge range this is no easy task, although counts at waterholes have gained useful results so far.

# Categories of Threat

The status categories that appear in the data panel for each species throughout this book are based on those published by the International Union for the Conservation of Nature (IUCN). They provide a useful guide to the current status of the species in the wild, and governments throughout the world use them when assessing conservation priorities and in policy-making. However, they do not provide automatic legal protection for the species.

Animals are placed in the appropriate category after scientific research. More species are being added all the time, and animals can be moved from one category to another as their circumstances change.

## Extinct (EX)

A group of animals is classified as EX when there is no reasonable doubt that the last individual has died.

## Extinct in the Wild (EW)

Animals in this category are known to survive only in captivity or as a population established artificially by introduction somewhere well outside its former range. A species is categorized as EW when exhaustive surveys throughout the areas where it used to occur consistently fail to record a single individual. It is important that such searches be carried out over all of the available habitat and during a season or time of day when the animals should be present.

## Critically Endangered (CR)

The category CR includes animals facing an extremely high risk of extinction in the wild in the immediate future. It includes any of the following:

- Any species with fewer than 50 individuals, even if the population is stable.
- Any species with fewer than 250 individuals if the population is declining, badly fragmented, or all in one vulnerable group.
- Animals from larger populations that have declined by 80 percent within 10 years (or are predicted to do so) or three generations, whichever is the longer.

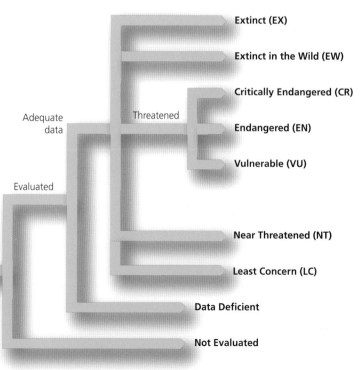

- Extinct (EX)
- Extinct in the Wild (EW)
- Critically Endangered (CR)
- Endangered (EN)
- Vulnerable (VU)
- Near Threatened (NT)
- Least Concern (LC)
- Data Deficient
- Not Evaluated

Adequate data — Threatened
Evaluated

**The IUCN categories**
*of threat. The system displayed has operated for new and reviewed assessments since January 2001.*

• Species living in a very small area—defined as under 39 square miles (100 sq. km).

### Endangered (EN)

A species is EN when it is not CR but is nevertheless facing a very high risk of extinction in the wild in the near future. It includes any of the following:

• A species with fewer than 250 individuals remaining, even if the population is stable.

• Any species with fewer than 2,500 individuals if the population is declining, badly fragmented, or all in one vulnerable subpopulation.

• A species whose population is known or expected to decline by 50 percent within 10 years or three generations, whichever is the longer.

• A species whose range is under 1,900 square miles (5,000 sq. km), and whose range, numbers, or population levels are declining, fragmented, or fluctuating wildly.

• Species for which there is a more than 20 percent likelihood of extinction in the next 20 years or five generations, whichever is the longer.

### Vulnerable (VU)

A species is VU when it is not CR or EN but is facing a high risk of extinction in the wild in the medium-term future. It includes any of the following:

• A species with fewer than 1,000 mature individuals remaining, even if the population is stable.

• Any species with fewer than 10,000 individuals if the population is declining, badly fragmented, or all in one vulnerable subpopulation.

• A species whose population is known, believed, or expected to decline by 20 percent within 10 years or

**Sport hunting**

*of white-headed ducks (this bird is a female) has been banned on two large Turkish lakes that have important wintering populations of the species.*

three generations, whichever is the longer.
• A species whose range is less than 772 square miles (20,000 sq. km), and whose range, numbers, or population structure are declining, fragmented, or fluctuating wildly.
• Species for which there is a more than 10 percent likelihood of extinction in the next 100 years.

## Near Threatened/Least Concern (since 2001)
In January 2001 the classification of lower-risk species was changed. Near Threatened (NT) and Least Concern (LC) were introduced as separate categories. They replaced the previous Lower Risk (LR) category with its subdivisions of Conservation Dependent (LRcd), Near Threatened (LRnt), and Least Concern (LRlc). From January 2001 all new assessments and reassessments must adopt NT or LC if relevant. But the older categories still apply to some animals until they are reassessed, and so are still in use.
• Near Threatened (NT)
Animals that do not qualify for CR, EN, or VU categories now but are close to qualifying or are likely to qualify for a threatened category in the future.
• Least Concern (LC)
Animals that have been evaluated and do not qualify for CR, EN, VU, or NT categories.

## Lower Risk (before 2001)
• Conservation Dependent (LRcd)
Animals whose survival depends on an existing conservation program
• Near Threatened (LRnt)

Animals for which there is no conservation program but that are close to qualifying for VU category.
• Least Concern (LRlc)

*By monitoring populations of threatened animals like this American rosy boa, biologists help keep the IUCN Red List up to date.*

*Conservation bodies now work with landholders to advise on the protection of grassland areas where gouldian finches breed in their native Australia.*

Species that are not conservation dependent or near threatened.

## Data Deficient (DD)
A species or population is DD when there is not enough information on abundance and distribution to assess the risk of extinction. In some cases, when the species is thought to live only in a small area, or a considerable period of time has passed since the species was last recorded, it may be placed in a threatened category as a precaution.

## Not Evaluated (NE)
Such animals have not yet been assessed.

**Note: a colored panel** in each entry in this book indicates the current level of threat to the species. The two new categories (NT and LC) and two of the earlier Lower Risk categories (LRcd and LRnt) are included within the band LR; the old LRlc is included along with Data Deficient (DD) and Not Evaluated (NE) under "Other," abbreviated to "O."

CITES *lists animals in the major groups in three Appendices, depending on the level of threat posed by international trade.*

| | Appendix I | Appendix II | Appendix III |
|---|---|---|---|
| **Mammals** | 277 species 16 subspecies 14 populations | 295 species 12 subspecies 12 populations | 45 species 8 subspecies |
| **Birds** | 152 species 11 subspecies 2 populations | 1,268 species 6 subspecies 1 populations | 35 species |
| **Reptiles** | 75 species 5 subspecies 6 populations | 527 species 4 subspecies 4 populations | 55 species |
| **Amphibians** | 16 species | 98 species | |
| **Fish** | 15 species | 71 species | |
| **Invertebrates** | 62 species 4 subspecies | 2,100 species 1 subspecies | 17 species |

## CITES APPENDICES

**Appendix I** lists the most endangered of traded species, namely those that are threatened with extinction and will be harmed by continued trade. These species are usually protected in their native countries and can only be imported or exported with a special permit. Permits are required to cover the whole transaction—both exporter and importer must prove that there is a compelling scientific justification for moving the animal from one country to another. This includes transferring animals between zoos for breeding purposes. Permits are only issued when it can be proved that the animal was legally acquired and that the remaining population will not be harmed by the loss.

**Appendix II** includes species that are not currently threatened with extinction, but that could easily become so if trade is not carefully controlled. Some common animals are listed here if they resemble endangered species so closely that criminals could try to sell the rare species pretending they were a similar common one. Permits are required to export such animals, with requirements similar to those Appendix I species.

**Appendix III** species are those that are at risk or protected in at least one country. Other nations may be allowed to trade in animals or products, but they may need to prove that they come from safe populations.

CITES designations are not always the same for every country. In some cases individual countries can apply for special permission to trade in a listed species. For example, they might have a safe population of an animal that is very rare elsewhere. Some African countries periodically apply for permission to export large quantities of elephant tusks that have been in storage for years, or that are the product of a legal cull of elephants. This is controversial because it creates an opportunity for criminals to dispose of black market ivory by passing it off as coming from one of those countries where elephant products are allowed to be exported. If you look up the African elephant, you will see that it is listed as CITES I, II, and III, depending on the country location of the different populations.

# Organizations

The human race is undoubtedly nature's worst enemy, but we can also help limit the damage caused by the rapid increase in our numbers and activities. There have always been people eager to protect the world's beautiful places and to preserve its most special animals, but it is only quite recently that the conservation message has begun to have a real effect on everyday life, government policy, industry, and agriculture.

Early conservationists were concerned with preserving nature for the benefit of people. They acted with an instinctive sense of what was good for nature and people, arguing for the preservation of wilderness and animals in the same way as others argued for the conservation of historic buildings or gardens. The study of ecology and environmental science did not really take off until the mid-20th century, and it took a long time for the true scale of our effect in the natural world to become apparent. Today the conservation of wildlife is based on far greater scientific understanding, but the situation has become much more complex and urgent in the face of human development.

By the mid-20th century extinction was becoming an immediate threat. Animals such as the passenger pigeon, quagga, and thylacine had disappeared despite last-minute attempts to save them. More and more species were discovered to be at risk, and species-focused conservation groups began to appear. In the early days there was little that any of these organizations could do but campaign against direct killing. Later they became a kind of conservation emergency service—rushing to the aid of seriously threatened animals in an attempt to save the species. But as time went on, broader environmental issues began to receive the urgent attention they needed. Research showed time and time again that saving species almost always comes down to addressing the

**Conservation** *organizations range from government departments in charge of national parks, such as Yellowstone National Park (right), the oldest in the United States, to local initiatives set up to protect endangered birds. Here (above) a man in Peru climbs a tree to check on the nest of a harpy eagle discovered near his village.*

problem of habitat loss. The world is short of space, and ensuring that there is enough for all the species is very difficult.

Conservation is not just about animals and plants, nor even the protection of whole ecological systems. Conservation issues are so broad that they touch almost every aspect of our lives, and successful measures often depend on the expertise of biologists, ecologists, economists, diplomats, lawyers, social scientists, and businesspeople. Conservation is all about cooperation and teamwork. Often it is also about helping people benefit from taking care of their wildlife. The organizations involved vary from small groups of a few dozen enthusiasts in local communities to vast, multinational operations.

"FOR THE BENEFIT AND ENJOYMENT OF THE PEOPLE"

## THE IUCN

With so much activity based in different countries, it is important to have a worldwide overview, some way of coordinating what goes on in different parts of the planet. That is the role of the International Union for the Conservation of Nature (IUCN), also referred to as the World Conservation Union. It began life as the International Union for the Preservation of Nature in 1948, becoming the IUCN in 1956. It is relatively new compared to the Sierra Club, Flora and Fauna International, and the Royal Society for the Protection of Birds. It was remarkable in that its founder members included governments, government agencies, and nongovernmental organizations. In the

years following the appalling destruction of World War II, the IUCN was born out of a desire to draw a line under the horrors of the past and to act together to safeguard the future.

The mission of the IUCN is to influence, encourage, and assist societies throughout the world to conserve the diversity of nature and natural systems. It seeks to ensure that the use of natural resources is fair and ecologically sustainable. Based in Switzerland, the IUCN has over 1,000 permanent staff and the help of 11,000 volunteer experts from about 180 countries. The work of the IUCN is split into six commissions, which deal with protected areas, policy-making, ecosystem management, education, environmental law, and species survival. The Species Survival Commission (SSC) has almost 7,000 members, all experts in the study of plants and animals. Within the SSC there are Specialist Groups concerned with the conservation of different types of animals, from cats to flamingos, deer, ducks, bats, and crocodiles. Some particularly well-studied animals, such as the African elephant and the polar bear, have their own specialist groups.

Perhaps the best-known role of the IUCN SSC is in the production of the Red Data Books, or Red Lists. First published in 1966, the books were designed to be easily updated, with details of each species on a different page that could be removed and replaced as new information came to light.

By 2010 the Red Lists include information on about 45,000 types of animal, of which almost 10,000 are threatened with extinction. Gathering this amount of information together is a

**The IUCN Red Lists** *of threatened species are published online and can be accessed at:*
*http://www.*
*iucnredlist.org*

huge task, but it provides an invaluable conservation resource. The Red Lists are continually updated and are now available on the World Wide Web. The Red Lists are the basis for the categories of threat used in this book.

## CITES

CITES is the Convention on International Trade in Endangered Species of Wild Fauna and Flora (also known as the Washington Convention, since it first came into force after an international meeting in Washington D.C. in 1973). Currently 175 nations have agreed to implement the CITES regulations. Exceptions to the convention include Iraq and North Korea, which, for the time being at least, have few trading links with the rest of the world. Trading in animals and their body parts has been a major factor in the decline of some of the world's rarest species. The IUCN categories draw attention to the status of rare species, but they do not confer any legal protection. That is done through national laws.

Conventions serve as international laws. In the case of CITES, lists (called Appendices) are agreed on internationally and reviewed every few years. The Appendices list the species that are threatened by international trade. Animals are assigned to Appendix I when all trade is forbidden. Any specimens of these species, alive or dead (or skins, feathers, etc.), will be confiscated by customs at international borders, seaports, or airports. Appendix II species can be traded internationally, but only under strict controls. Wildlife trade is often valuable in the rural economy, and this raises difficult questions about the relative importance of animals and people. Nevertheless, traders who ignore CITES rules risk heavy fines or imprisonment. Some rare species—even those with the highest IUCN categories (many bats and frogs, for example)—may have no CITES protection simply because they have no commercial value. Trade is then not really a threat.

**The Greenpeace ship,** *seen here in Antarctica, travels to areas of conservation concern and helps draw worldwide media attention to environmental issues.*

## WILDLIFE CONSERVATION ORGANIZATIONS

### BirdLife International
BirdLife International is a partnership of 60 organizations working in more than 100 countries. Most partners are national nongovernmental conservation groups such as the Canadian Nature Federation. Others include large bird charities such as the Royal Society for the Protection of Birds in Britain. By working together within BirdLife International, even small organizations can be effective globally as well as on a local scale. BirdLife International is a member of the IUCN.
Web site: http://www.birdlife.org

### Conservation International (CI)
Founded in 1987, Conservation International works closely with the IUCN and has a similar multinational approach. CI offers help in the world's most threatened biodiversity hot spots.
Web site: http://conservation.org

### Durrell Wildlife Conservation Trust (DWCT)
Another IUCN member, the Durrell Wildlife Conservation Trust was founded by the British naturalist and author Gerald Durrell in 1963. The trust is based at Durrell's world-famous zoo on Jersey in the Channel Islands. Jersey was the world's first zoo dedicated solely to the conservation of endangered species. Breeding programs at the zoo have helped stabilize populations of some of the world's most endangered animals. The trust trains conservationists from many countries and works to secure areas of natural habitat to which animals can be returned. Jersey Zoo and the DWCT were instrumental in saving numerous species from extinction, including the pink pigeon, Mauritius kestrel, Waldrapp ibis, St. Lucia parrot, and the Telfair's skink and other reptiles.
Web site: http://durrell.org

### Fauna & Flora International (FFI)
Founded in 1903, this organization has had various name changes. It began life as a society for protecting large mammals, but has broadened its scope. It was involved in saving the Arabian oryx from extinction.
Web site: http://www.fauna-flora.org

### National Audubon Society
John James Audubon was an American naturalist and wildlife artist who died in 1851, 35 years before the society that bears his name was founded. The first Audubon Society was established by George Bird Grinnell in protest against the appalling overkill of birds for meat, feathers, and sport. By the end of the 19th century there were Audubon Societies in 15 states, and they later became part of the National Audubon Society, which funds scientific research programs, publishes

# WILDLIFE CONSERVATION ORGANIZATIONS

magazines and journals, manages wildlife sanctuaries, and advises state and federal governments on conservation issues.
Web site: http://www.audubon.org

### Pressure Groups

Friends of the Earth, founded in Britain in 1969, and Greenpeace, founded in 1971 in British Columbia, were the first environmental pressure groups to become internationally recognized. Greenpeace became known for "direct, nonviolent actions," which drew attention to major conservation issues. (For example, campaigners steered boats between the harpoon guns of whalers and their prey.)

The organizations offer advice to governments and corporations, and help those that seek to protect the environment, while continuing to name, shame, and campaign against those who do not.

### Royal Society for the Protection of Birds

This organization was founded in the 1890s to campaign against the slaughter of birds to supply feathers for the fashion trade. It now has a wider role and has become Britain's premier wildlife conservation organization, with over a million members. It is involved in international activities, particularly in the protection of birds that migrate to Britain.
Web site: http://www.rspb.org.uk

### The Sierra Club

The Sierra Club was started in 1892 by John Muir and is still going strong. Muir, a Scotsman by birth, is often thought of as the founder of the conservation movement, especially in the United States, where he campaigned for the preservation of wilderness. It was through his efforts that the first national parks, including Yosemite,

Sequoia, and Mount Rainier, were established. Today the Sierra Club remains dedicated to the preservation of wild places for the benefit of wildlife and the enjoyment of people.
Web site: http://www.sierraclub.org

### World Wide Fund for Nature (WWF)

The World Wide Fund for Nature, formerly the World Wildlife Fund, was born in 1961. It was a joint venture between the IUCN, several existing conservation organizations, and a number of successful businesspeople. Unlike many charities, WWF was big, well-funded, and high profile from the beginning. Its familiar giant panda emblem ranks alongside those of the Red Cross, Mercedes Benz, or Coca-Cola in terms of instant international recognition.
Web site: http://www.wwf.org

# GLOSSARY

**adaptation** Features of an animal that adjust it to its environment; may be produced by evolution–e.g., camouflage coloration

**adaptive radiation** Where a group of closely related animals (e.g., members of a family) have evolved differences from each other so that they can survive in different niches

**bill** Often called the beak: the jaws of a bird, consisting of two bony mandibles, upper and lower, and their horny sheaths

**biodiversity** The variety of species and the variation within them

**biome** A major world landscape characterized by having similar plants and animals living in it, e.g., desert, rain forest, forest

**breeding season** The entire cycle of reproductive activity, from courtship, pair formation (and often establishment of territory) through nesting to independence of young

**bristle** In birds a modified feather, with a bare or partly bare shaft, like a stiff hair; functions include protection, as with eyelashes of ostriches and hornbills, and touch sensors to help catch insects, as with flycatchers

**brood** The young hatching from a single clutch of eggs

**carrion** Rotting flesh of dead animals

**casque** The raised portion on the head of certain reptiles and birds

**class** A large taxonomic group of related animals. Mammals, insects, and reptiles are all classes of animals

**cloaca** Cavity in the pelvic region into which the alimentary canal, and the genital and urinary ducts open

**clutch** A set of eggs laid by a female bird in a single breeding attempt

**coverts** Small feathers covering the bases of a bird's main flight feathers on the wings and tail, providing a streamlined surface for flight

**DNA** (deoxyribonucleic acid) The substance that makes up the main part of the chromosomes of all living things; contains the genetic code that is handed down from generation to generation

**down** Soft, fluffy, insulating feathers with few or no shafts found after hatching on young birds and in adults beneath the main feathers

**ecology** The study of plants and animals in relation to one another and their surroundings

**ecosystem** A whole system in which plants, animals, and their environment interact

**ectotherm** Animal that relies on external heat sources to raise body temperature; also known as "cold-blooded"

**endemic** Found only in one geographical area, nowhere else

**eutrophication** An increase in the nutrient chemicals (nitrates, phosphates, etc.) in water, sometimes occurring naturally and sometimes caused by human activities, e.g., by the release of sewage or agricultural fertilizers

**family** A group of closely related genera that often also look similar. Zoological family names always end in -idae. Also used to describe a social group within a species comprising parents and their offspring

**fledging period** The period between a young bird hatching and acquiring its first full set of feathers and being able to fly

**fledgling** Young bird that is capable of flight; in perching birds and some others it corresponds with the time of leaving the nest

**gene** The basic unit of heredity, enabling one generation to pass on characteristics to its offspring

**genus** (genera, pl.) A group of closely related species

**hybrid** Offspring of two closely related species that can breed; it is sterile and so cannot produce offspring

**incubation** The act of keeping the egg or eggs warm or the period from the laying of eggs to hatching

**insectivore** An animal that feeds on insects. Also sometimes used as a group name for hedgehogs, shrews, moles, etc.

**interbreeding** Breeding between animals of different species, varieties, etc. within a single family or strain; interbreeding can cause dilution of the gene pool

**iridescent** Displaying glossy colors produced (e.g., in bird plumage) not as a result of pigments but by the splitting of sunlight into light of different wavelengths; rainbows are made in the same way

**keratin** Tough, fibrous material that forms hair, feathers, nails, and protective plates on the skin of vertebrate animals

**lek** Communal display area where male birds gather to attract and mate with females

**mandible** Upper or lower part of a bird's beak or bill

**migration** Movement from one place to another and back again; usually seasonal

**molt** The process in which a bird sheds its feathers and replaces them with new ones

**nestling** A young bird still in the nest and dependent on its parents

**omnivore** An animal that eats a wide range of both animal and vegetable food

**ornithologist** Zoologist specializing in the study of birds

**passerine** Any bird of the order Passeriformes; includes songbirds

**plume** A long feather used for display, as in a bird of paradise

**polygamous** Where an individual has more than one mate in one breeding season. Monogamous animals have only a single mate

**polygynous** Where a male mates with several females in one breeding season

**primary forest** Forest that has always been forest and has not been cut down and regrown at some time

**raptor** Bird with hooked beak and strong feet with sharp claws (talons) for seizing, killing, and dealing with prey; also known as birds of prey.

**regurgitate** (of a bird) To vomit partly digested food either to feed nestlings or to rid itself of bones, fur, or other indigestible parts, or (in some seabirds) to scare off predators

**scapulars** The feathers of a bird above its shoulders

**secondary forest** Trees that have been planted or have grown up on cleared ground

**speciation** The origin of species; the diverging of two similar organisms through reproduction down through the generations into different forms resulting in a new species

**species** A group of animals that look similar and can breed with each other to produce fertile offspring. A subspecies is a subpopulation of a single species whose members differ from the typical form for that species; sometimes called a race

**vane** The bladelike main part of a typical bird feather extending from either side of its shaft (midrib)

**wattle** Fleshy protuberance, usually near the base of a bird's bill

**wingbar** Line of contrasting feathers on a bird's wing

**yolk** Part of the egg that contains nourishment for a growing embryo

# FURTHER RESEARCH

## Books

### Birds
Attenborough, David, *The Life of Birds,* BBC Books, London, U.K., 1998

BirdLife International, *Threatened Birds of the World*, Lynx Edicions, Barcelona, Spain and BirdLife International, Cambridge, U.K., 2000

del Hoyo, J., Elliott, A., and Sargatal, J., eds., *Handbook of Birds of the World Vols 1 to 15,* Lynx Edicions, Barcelona, Spain, 1992–2010

Dunn, Jon, and Alderfer, Jonathan K., *National Geographic Field Guide to the Birds of North America,* National Geographic Society, Washington D.C., United States, 2006.

Stattersfield, A., Crosby, M., Long, A., and Wege, D., eds., *Endemic Bird Areas of the World: Priorities for Biodiversity Conservation,* BirdLife International, Cambridge, U.K., 1998

### Mammals
Macdonald, David, *The New Encyclopedia of Mammals,* Oxford University Press, Oxford, U.K., 2009

Payne, Roger, *Among Whales*, Bantam Press, U.S., 1996

Reeves, R. R., and Leatherwood, S., *The Sierra Club Handbook of Whales and Dolphins of the World*, Sierra Club, U.S., 1983

Sherrow, Victoria, and Cohen, Sandee, *Endangered Mammals of North America*, Twenty-First Century Books, U.S., 1995

Whitaker, J. O., Audubon Society *Field Guide to North American Mammals,* Alfred A. Knopf, New York, U.S., 1996

Wilson, Don E., Mittermeier, Russell A., *Handbook of Mammals of the World Vol 1,* Lynx Edicions, Barcelona, Spain, 2009

### Fish
Buttfield, Helen, *The Secret Lives of Fishes*, Abrams, U.S., 2000

Dawes, John, and Campbell, Andrew, eds., *The New Encyclopedia of Aquatic Life, Facts On File*, New York, U.S., 2004

### Reptiles and Amphibians
Corbett, Keith, *Conservation of European Reptiles and Amphibians,* Christopher Helm, London, U.K., 1989

Corton, Misty, *Leopard and Other South African Tortoises,* Carapace Press, London, U.K., 2000

Hofrichter, Robert, *Amphibians: The World of Frogs, Toads, Salamanders, and Newts*, Firefly Books, Canada, 2000

Murphy, J. B., Adler, K., and Collins, J. T. (eds.), *Captive Management and Conservation of Reptiles and Amphibians*, Society for the Study of Amphibians and Reptiles, Ithaca, New York, 1994

Stafford, Peter, *Snakes*, Natural History Museum, London, U.K., 2000

### Insects
Eaton, Eric R. and Kaufman, Kenn. *Kaufman Field Guide to Insects of North America*, Houghton Mifflin, New York, U.S., 2007

Pyle, Robert Michael, National Audubon Society *Field Guide to North American Butterflies*, Pyle, Robert Michael, A. Knopf, New York, U.S., 1995

### General
Allaby, Michael, *A Dictionary of Ecology*, Oxford University Press, New York, U.S., 2010

Douglas, Dougal, and others, *Atlas of Life on Earth*, Barnes & Noble, New York, U.S., 2001

## Web sites
http://www.nature.nps.gov/ U.S. National Park Service wildlife site

http://www.abcbirds.org/ American Bird Conservancy. Articles, information about bird conservation in the Americas

http://www.ummz.lsa.umich-edu/umich.edu/ University of Michigan Museum of Zoology animal diversity web. Search for pictures and information about animals by class, family, and common name

http://www.audubon.org National Audubon Society. Sections on education, local societies, and bird identification

http://www.birdlife.org BirdLife International, an alliance of conservation organizations working in over 100 countries to save birds and their habitats

http://www.birds.cornell.edu/ Cornell University. Courses, news, nest-box cam

http://www.cites.org/ CITES and IUCN listings. Search for animals by order, family, genus, species, or common name. Location by country and explanation of reasons for listings

http://www.cmc-ocean.org Facts, figures, and quizzes about marine life

www.darwinfoundation.org/ Charles Darwin Research Center

http://www.fws.gov.endangered Information about endangered animals and plants from the U.S. Fish and Wildlife Service, the organization in charge of 94 million acres of wildlife refuges

http://www.endangeredspecie.com Information, links, books, and publications about rare and endangered species. Also includes information about conservation efforts and organizations

http://www.ewt.org.za Endangered South African wildlife

http://forests.org/ Includes forest conservation answers to queries

http://www.iucn.org Details of species, IUCN listings, and IUCN publications. Link to online Red Lists of threatened species at: www.iucnredlist.org

http://www.open.ac.uk/daptf/ DAPTF–Declining Amphibian Population Task Force. Provides information and data about amphibian declines

# INDEX

Words and page numbers in **bold type** indicate main references to the various topics.

## A

Algeria 16, 19
Alkaline lakes 15
Amazonia 38
Andean flamingo **14–15**
Andes Mountains 15
Antarctic 4, 34
Aransas National Wildlife Refuge, Texas 32
Arctic 4
Atlantic Ocean 12, 50
'Aversion training' 29
Avian malaria 5
Australia 46, 52

## B

Bee hummingbird **44–45**
Bermuda 12
Bermuda petrel **12–13**
Blue bird of paradise **48–49**
Bolivia 38
Brazil 6, 38
Britain 19, 26

## C

California 28, 42
California condor **28–29**
Canada 32, 33, 42
Cats 8, 11, 21, 30, 34, 36, 37, 40, 51
Cape Verde Islands 26, 50, 51
Captive breeding programs 17, 19, 23, 28, 29, 31, 33, 35
Caribbean 13
Caspian Sea 18
Chile 10
Colombia 6
Cuba 44, 45

## D

DDT 13
Diatoms 14
Dinosaurs 5
Disease 25, 31, 40, 41
Dogs 8, 11, 20, 34, 36, 51
Drought 15, 16, 32, 51

## E

Ecuador 6
Electrocution 25
El Nino 11
England 27
Eradication program 19
Eucalypts/eucalyptus 46, 52
Eutrophication 18

## F

Florida 33
Forest clearance 8, 22
Foxes 34
France 19

## G

Galápagos Islands 10, 11
Galápagos penguin **10–11**
Global warming 5, 11, 13
Gouldian finch **52–53**
Grazing 47, 53

## H

Habitat loss 8, 42, 47, 49
Hawaii 20, 21
Heat transfer system 10

## I

Important Bird Areas (IBAs) 7
Indian Ocean 30

## K

Kakapo **36–37**
Kazakhstan 19

## L

Logging 22, 45, 47

## M

Mauritius 30, 31, 40
Mauritius kestrel **30–31**
Mexico 28
Middle East 16
Migration 4
Mongoose 20, 21, 40
Morocco 16, 17, 18, 24, 25
Myxomatosis 25

## N

Natural disasters 23
Nectar 44, 46, 47
Nene **20–21**
Nest boxes 39
New Guinea 46, 48, 49
New Zealand 8, 34, 36
New York Zoological Society 40
North Africa 16
Northern bald ibis **16–17**
Northern brown kiwi **8–9**

## O

Oceania 6
Oil spills 11

## P

Pacific Ocean 6, 34, 42
Pantanal 38, 39
Paraguay 38
Parasitic mite 53
Peru 10
Pesticides 16, 17, 23, 26
Philippine eagle **22–23**
Philippines 22
Pink pigeon **40–41**
Poisoning 25, 26, 28, 29
Pollution 15, 18, 32
Portugal 19, 24, 25
Possums 34, 36
*Pterodroma* petrels 12
Puna 14

## R

Rabbits 25, 26, 34
Raso lark **50–51**
Ratites 8
Rats 11, 20, 30, 34, 36, 40, 51
Red kite **26–27**
Regent honeyeater **46–47**
Ruddy duck 19
Russia 19

## S

Scotland 27
Self-sustaining population 32, 33, 35
Slash-and-burn agriculture 23, 45
Spain 18, 19, 24, 25, 27
Spanish imperial eagle **24–25**
Spotted owl **42–43**
Stoats 8, 34, 35, 36
Subsistence agriculture 49
Sweden 27

## T

Takahe **34–35**
Trapping 39
Tubenose 13
Tuberculosis 14
Turkey 16, 18, 19

## U

United States 11, 28, 38, 42, 43

## W

Wales 26, 27
Water extraction 18
White-headed duck **18–19**
Whooping crane **32–33**
Wildfowl and Wetlands Trust 21
Wisconsin 32
Wood Buffalo National Park, Canada 32
World Center for Birds of Prey 28, 31
World Wide Fund for Nature 40